Girl, Get Your Mind Right!

Girl, Get Your Mind Right!

Tionna Tee Smalls

iUniverse, Inc.
New York Lincoln Shanghai

Girl, Get Your Mind Right!

iUniverse books may be ordered through booksellers or by contacting:

iUniverse
2021 Pine Lake Road, Suite 100
Lincoln, NE 68512
www.iuniverse.com
1-800-Authors (1-800-288-4677)

Because of the dynamic nature of the Internet, any Web addresses
or links contained in this book may have changed
since publication and may no longer be valid.

The views expressed in this work are solely those of the author and do
not necessarily reflect the views of the publisher, and the publisher
hereby disclaims any responsibility for them

ISBN: 978-0-595-45402-0 (pbk)
ISBN: 978-0-595-89715-5 (ebk)

Printed in the United States of America

This book is dedicated to my 3rd grade teacher, Mrs. Janet Smith, for always believing in me.

Contents

Acknowledgements

This is my chance to say thank you to all the people in my past, present, and future that have motivated me and stood by my side. I like to think of this page as more of a shout out page because no matter where this book takes me I would never forget about the people that made my life the best that it could possibly be.

First of all I would like to thank God for being my savior, for always helping me through my trials and tribulations, and for giving me the talent and motivation that I have today. Thank you Jesus, I know I am not the biggest Christian in the world but hey, I am working on it. Secondly, I would like to thank my parents who gave me life under that Christmas tree oh so many years ago. I thank my mother for always sticking by my side and believing in me whether I wanted to sew, paint, do real estate agent, or write a book. I want to thank my father for always keeping me strong and telling me that he didn't want any of his daughters to be weak. Daddy T, you had a lot of crazy ways of teaching us but I guessed it work. I also want to thank you for being for being the love of my mother's life especially after Grandma and Grandpa died. I know were always going to fight but I love you, always did and always will despite what you may think.

I would like to thank my sisters: Toni, Bunny, and Honey for always making me want to do right in my life. Toni, I am glad everything is going great for you in your life. Bunny, you are a strong and beautiful young lady and we didn't always get along but we are sisters and we must always look out for each other and I think you're the best mom ever. Honey, you are really strong and I really admire that. You watched me very well but only you're worse. Keep your attitude! I love you.

I want to give shout outs to my family: Grandma Showie, Godmother Barbara Johnson, Aunt Mary, Uncle Gary, Meak, Tiff, Man, Audrey, Lavon, Tasha, Little Gary and Tommy, Donald, Tobias, King Easter, Tai-Jae, Aunt Tanya, Uncle June, Aunt Dorothy, Tiwauna, Monique, Uncle Lorenzo, Aunt Tracey, Trey, Michael and Marquita Jones, Laurel and Darryl Gause, Uncle Harry, Uncle Ricky,

I would like to thank my friends (past and present): Lovell Nimmons, Ryan Exum, Elaina Whyte, Michelle Gilyard, Michelle Hunt, Shelly, Laura Yarborough,

Kurt Lindsay, Jason Gray, Low, Dave, James, Gloria and Neisha Rogers, Rob, Greg, Randy, Lashay and Lashauna Carr, Zalika Headley, Shatonya Perry, Tyquan Wright, Earl Cooper, Michael McCray, Reggie-O, Diamonte, Mr. Graham, Tayo, Araminta, Shavon, Simone, Genera, Knoelle, Samantha, Michael Hill, Dajuan Henderson, Anthony Brown, and Rodney and Felicia Exum, Gary Jones, Nelson Lee, Hassan Randall, Rakem Kato, Ramon Zanders, Lashawnda, Ant, Devine, Miggity, Tiauna, Naja, Tina, and the Alexander family.

To the motivators of my life: Prof. Cole, Prof. Perrea, Dana Oberfest, Jason Esposito, Janet Smith, and I would like to thank the East New York Community, Kevin McCall, and all my college mates. R.I.P—Lillian Wise, Brenda Lee Smalls, Michelle Gomez, and Darrell Wilson. If I forgot you, please blame my mind and not my heart. Thank you and God Bless.

Foreword

Girl, Get Your Mind Right! Is the unsupported opinion of Tionna Tee Smalls. Tionna Tee Smalls is not a psychologist but has been watching women and relationships since she was 12-years-old. Every point that is made in this book has been studied carefully. This book was written from experience with the intent to motivate women. This book is about the hardships that women may face in life while dealing with men. *Girl, Get Your Mind Right!* Is for the woman that is tired of the bullcrap and ready to say "No more cheating", "No more lies", and "No more putting a man before myself." This book breaks down the issues and makes us all think about why certain things happen in a relationship. *Girl, Get Your Mind Right!* Is also great for entertainment purposes as well and was written by the author during an angry time in her life

Introduction: What's Messing up Your Mind?

A "mind wrecker" is a man who will do anything to mess up your soul and make you feel low. He is manipulator, a liar, and overall a game player. You have been dealing with this man for over 2 years and still you don't know your place in his heart. He compliments you sometimes to cover his real jealousy that he has against you. He will take any chance that he has to make you feel down (psychologically). If everyone he knows thinks you're so great, he would find a way to let them know that you're just as average as his last girlfriend. This Mind Wrecker will make you feel like you're his queen in front of other people but when you two are alone he does little things that make you wonder what is his true intentions for you. This is a man who wants you all to himself without any family or close friends around that can catch him on his bullshit.

This Mind Wrecker may not physically put his hands on you but he will verbally bash you in every argument that you have by calling you a slut, a whore, a side bitch, an ugly bitch, a fat bitch, etc. This Mind Wrecker knows that you're a good catch and secretly admires your drive, your motivation, your confidence, but all the while he hates you for those same qualities. This man wants to break down that box to get to your brain so that he can take over and conquer you. He only wants to get back with you after a breakup when he feels that you're on top and you could live your life without him.

He will come back to your world and make you think he's a changed man only to do the same thing he has done to you just a month ago.

This man loves the way you look but will still go and screw an ugly girl on the side just for kicks. This man loves to see you cry and love to hear you talk smack about other people who are in your life. He will urge you on even more to get rid of your friends so that he could have the upper hand and therefore be the only source to your heart, happiness, and laughter. He will want you to come home after work and not have a drink with the girls but will be the first person that will break his dinner date with you just to go chilling with his boys. He never lets you know his plans ahead of time because doesn't want you to know his every move.

This Mind Wrecker seems confident on the outside but inside he really doesn't feel worthy of you and knows that he's not your level, so he will try to knock you down a notch so that you and him can be on the same ground. All he does is bring havoc to your once peaceful life because he likes to see you fight emotionally and physically for his love and you like the Sweetheart that you are will recognize these signs and work with him hoping it wouldn't be like this is forever and the very sad thing is that he is never going to change.

He will screw your emotions up so much that you will not be the nice quiet girl you once were. You will be a mad bitch to everyone around you however you will still bow down and take his bullcrap because that is the way he has trained you to be. Before you dated him, you saw life as one big, beautiful, adventurous place. If you didn't get something you wanted, you said, "Oh well, let me try again" but after messing with this negative Tot the glass is no longer half full to you, it's half empty and you see everything as one big black hole. You begin to get frustrated while trying to accomplish the smallest task and you will start to question yourself and wonder if anything is worth trying.

He makes you so paranoid that every time he's away from you, you believe he is doing something sexual with another female. He loves when he gets you crazy like that so he will play on it even more by not answering his phone and pretending to be sleep when you call only to piss your whole night and early morning off. Therefore, you go to work, upset, and worried about what's he doing and not focused on what you're supposed to be focused on—your money. That headache and cry fest you had on his voicemail is his confirmation that he is going to be on your mind all day. He is a Mind Wrecker so he likes taking over the only place that you can't control because believe it or not, you can't control what you think about; he knows this and loves every minute of it. Then what comes next is a phone call or stupid text saying, *you know I love you, why would I hurt you?* Then you two make plans to meet and talk after work only for him to be back in your bed penetrating your vagina. He's groaning and telling you sweet nothings in your ear all the while trying to get a nut and think of another master of disaster plan on how to get your fine ass off of that plateau that you always seem to be on.

See, nothing changes but the game and he knows when you're crying during this love session and promising him that you're not going to go anywhere that he's fucking not only your body but your mind as well. He knows that he's still in charge even though you are on top riding his dick like it's the last thing smoking. And why is he control? Because were women and we wear our heart on our sleeves and many times we mistake sex for love and get gassed up by those 4 letter words especially during intimacy. Why else is he in charge? Because he understands that in any love relationship, there is the Lover (the person who gives the love) which is you and there is the Beloved (the person who receives the love) which is him. He knows that you would do anything for him and that no matter how much he messes up; you're going take him back after he begs for your forgiveness and be a good boy for a week or two.

This manipulator doesn't love you; hell, he barely takes you seriously. He just wants to get in where he fits in just like everybody else and it's no longer about sex, please he's been screwing since he was 13-years-old. It's about winning over someone who everyone else claims is the star in the relationship. Getting you used to be the prize for him now destroying you is. He may smile like he believes in you and may taste the inside of your walls but he's waiting for your down fall so that once you're down he could step all over you and make you feel like you never had any existence in his world in the first place. He would now look at you as the person who once tried to oppressed him and make him feel unworthy with your achievements. He will try to impregnate you only to convince you to have an abortion, knowing that going through that procedure will hurt you more mentally and physically than having the baby itself.

Welcome to the sick world of the man who sleeps with you every night, been with you for years, but still cant stand your freaking guts. It's him, the Mind Wrecker. You're loving him, you're co-signing his bullshit, but most of all you're fucking him! So ladies, without further interruptions, let's get our mind right!

It's All About You

Growing up as a little girl with parents who were happily married and who most of the females in her family had companions, I didn't know or discover what it was like to be alone. I barely ever saw women alone and if they were, they were labeled as a whore or as a miserable bitch. These "lonely" women were the talk of almost every one of my family's barbeques. It was like if Tricia, who didn't bring a date, wore those tight white jean shorts with that "wife beater" that hugged her breast walked by and all my Uncles were standing there talking shit about the Lakers game with a Heineken in their had when she walked by and they got quiet, she was the talk of the event. "Look at that lonely bitch," or the all time favorite, "She think she's cute," that would be what is said about her from all the married or the involved women.

I think my Aunts may have been jealous of the sexual energy that a Tricia may have possessed or maybe it was the fact that she was dateless and still seemed to be enjoying herself at what seemed to be a couples-only event. I learned a lot about women from observing situations like this one. What I now ask myself is, did they consider her to be miserable because she was alone? I thought that maybe it was more socially expected for a woman to have a man. What I wonder is, when did this all began? Why are the Tricias of the world the talk of the town? Are women jealous of other women who are smart, attractive, and exude confidence although they don't have a man or is it that such a beautiful woman who is unattached is intimidating to have around your man? Do women look at single women and automatically think of her as just another bitch out to steal their man or is there something that we are all lacking within ourselves?

From 15 to 21-years-old, I was involved in a relationship with one man. I often got kudos for that especially from the women in my family. I guess they were so impressed with the fact that we stayed together through puberty, schoolwork, basketball groupies, and peer pressure. I don't know how but somehow we made it work. Anyway, my first love, Rahmel, and I were always invited to many outings together because I guess since I was involved in a happy relationship I wasn't a threat and life was good. People always wanted me to go out with them because I was in love and I wasn't even thinking about another man no matter what game he tried to spit that night. I would go out, dance, hold conversations, and laugh but behaved myself because I knew what I had at home (see, a real woman never tries to mess up a good thing).

Anyway, I was the source of advice when someone had problems with their man. They came to me for advice because hey, I was the one in this long ass relationship but you know what like all good things in life, it all came to an end; Rahmel and I broke up due to what they call irreconcilable differences. I guess I became a victim of Relationship us versus them. You know how that goes, if you aint us then you got to be them (them meaning the single heffas). So the invitations to go partying began to stop little by little. All of a sudden now that I was single nobody wanted Tionna Smalls to go out with them; I was no longer the reliable source to come to when you were having problems with your man.

Don't get me wrong, I understand why people think you shouldn't ask a single person for advice; however, that saying goes for women who really never had a man. You cant tell me how to take care of something your ass never had; that's like asking a person who never had a pet in their whole life, how to groom and take care of a dog. Of course, they wouldn't know, they have never had a pet or had one long enough to know but once you have had something for 6 years, I think you should know what you are talking about.

I may have had a different breed of dog but I had one. Experience is something that never goes away but anyway, they stopped asking me for my advice. They started dictating what I should do just because I was now single. All of a sudden they were telling me that I should watch out for this person or that person but they were boning every Tom, Dick, and Harry before that dude from jail decided to marry their ass (yeah, everyone is an expert now). Ladies, we all know that when you have a man all your friends are single. They may date from time to time but no one serious but when your ass is single and lonely, honey, you're in a class all by yourself. All of a sudden everybody's exes are coming back in the midst and they're baby daddies are acting right, but don't worry! You have one friend and it doesn't matter what religion you believe in or whether you believe in a higher power or not, it's yourself.

I want you to remember that besides God, when chips are down, all you have is yourself. I'm with me 24 hours a day, 7 days a week and no matter what I say or do, there is no escaping me unless I commit suicide and I am definitely not doing that. Ladies, you have to remember that you're the most important person in your life because when it's all said and done, you will be alone. You were born by yourself, goddamn it, so bets to believe that you're going to die by yourself. There is not one person in this world that is going to jump in that casket with you, not even your Mama. You have to remember that your mind and body is what defines you. We all have different approaches to self-love and no, I am not talking about Mr. Jelly Chocolate, that plastic, black, penis shaped vibrator that you have under your bed. I am talking about real love. Love for yourself that you couldn't even imagine having.

The longer that I am alone, the more I realize that I like me. I like my short hair, I like my long neck, and I like the cellulite on my ass (ok, I'm pushing it a little bit) but you get my point. I realize now that all of my qualities whether they're good or bad are what makes me the person that I am today. In life, we women get so involved with these men, these friends, this money, that we are not realizing the destruction were doing to ourselves until it's too late. There are a lot of women out there that we look at as the bomb but they don't feel that way about themselves because they are lacking self-love. One may confuse like for self for love for self and believe me, there's a huge difference.

Women these days are looking for love in all the wrong places. We are looking to men, clothes, money, drugs, prostitution, sexual activity, etc to feel that love that were missing within ourselves and when it's all said and done, we feel worse than we did before. As women we have to find this love and keep it; hide it in a box and keep it only for ourselves and for the people in our lives who we feel deserves it. There is an old saying that we have all heard before, "you can't love nobody till you love you," and believe me kids, it's the truth. Remember, when you don't love yourself, you settle for anything that people throw at you and that right there is not cool.

Everyone around you could tell when you love yourself. When you love yourself, you just walk differently, you talk differently, and you possess a hidden glow that everybody could feel when they are around you. It's the feeling of smiling just because the sun seems to be glistening on you. Its like positive rays are coming out of your body and touching everything around you. One may ask how do you get this self-love? And believe me, one has asked me. The first person that asked me this was a 21-year-old Spanish male named Mario, who I went to college with. He was pretty handsome; tall, around six feet, light caramel, nice haircut, and a body straight out of the gym. He seemed to be fine but the "Psychiatrist" in me saw that he had problems with his self-confidence when he said, "I just want to be loved."

The way he said that made me say, "You want love because you're missing something within yourself," and he kindly agreed with me. "Maybe, you are right, maybe I don't love myself," he said. "How do I begin to love myself?" When he asked that question, a bell seemed to go off in my head. You know that same bell that goes off in your head when somebody asks you about a subject that you think you know a lot about. The question really intrigued me for numerous reasons. It intrigued me for one, because a man was asking it and in this world we ladies, yes a lot of us, assume men don't have self-esteem problems and for two because I just figured out around that same time what loving myself really was.

I was always confident about me but I realized after my breakup with my first love that I didn't really love myself at all. How did I know that? You ask. I know it because someone that loves themselves would never allow themselves to gain around fifty pounds during a relationship. One wouldn't of downed themselves so much and cared more about their man's future more than they did there own. Another way you could tell that you don't love yourself is when you don't do anything for yourself outside of a man. You don't love yourself when you don't go out there and try better yourself; you just live your life for other people. Not loving yourself does not solely have something to do with a man but it have a lot to do with one.

See, everyone has known a man who could make them feel like they aint shit. You know, you be feeling all fly; like you got the world in your hand and then this one dude come along and messes up how you feel about yourself with just one look. If this sounds familiar to you and you are still dealing with this man, you need to get him out of your life (quickly). It's sad but a lot of us women depend on men for that security, that feeling, overall that love that were missing with in. I understand that there are a lot of women out there who never grew up with a father but ladies, we have to stop making that our excuse to why we let these dudes come along and shit on us.

Loving yourself means never allowing someone to do you dirty and always nipping something in the butt before it gets way out of hand. There's something I always tell everyone of my friends when they're going through some questionable self esteem problems regarding their man—*Make him understand that its all about you.* Teaching him this does not take a lot, it just takes the strength to let a dude know that you will leave him where he's standing if he doesn't shape it up because you really don't need his bullcrap; straight up!

Now back to the question, how do you get it back? First rule in loving anyone, you have to spend time. Yes, girlfriend. Start spending some quality t-i-m-e with yourself for yourself. After I went through my little depression from the breakup with my first, I began to spend a whole lot of time with me. I started to go home more often after work and stayed in my room and just sat on my bed in thought. I turned my phone off, yes phones off and televisions definitely off because TV's influence you in both a positive and negative way. *The Fabulous Life Of* is the last thing you need to see when you're depressed about money or anything else that life brings along. So cut the TV's off and just sit there. Don't do this for just a day or two do this for a while and when you began to do this, you will realize what you have and what you don't have. You will realize your wants and desires and most of all, your *faults*.

You will only realize your faults if you're serious about change. Realizing your faults is like one step towards what I call *Self-Esteem Recovery*. When I sat down, I realized all the things that I didn't like about myself, and not only material things but internal/mental things as well, things that I could not control. I realized that I did not like how I always told people my personal business and I didn't like how I always kept grudges when someone did something wrong to me. Then I started to think harder. I started seeing that I didn't like many things about myself. I then began to get excited thinking of the things I could have done to relieve myself from those same problems.

See we could talk about our problems until the roosters come home but that's not intriguing any of us. Figuring out the solutions to your problems is what is mind blowing. So once you find out these resolutions, you're supposed to figure out a plan to better yourself and stick to it. The best advice I could give you is to get a composition notebook, an electronic device, or anything you can jot your thoughts on. Writing down your thoughts will be the savior of your life besides from your religious support (if you have any) because it helps you identify the issues that you may have never thought you had. Writing is the first step to loving yourself, believe me, it works! It's like having a diary. Remember those diaries that were out in the early 90's that you had your own key to? Didn't that diary help you figure out your life even though then your ass was just talking about what boy may have or may have not liked you and how you didn't like Gina because she was wearing a bra and you weren't? Life may have changed but the topics stayed the same. Were still complaining about that guy not showing us any attention and Gina is now making more money than us and rocking all the hottest fashions (well that's hating but I'm sure you get my gist).

The second way to get yourself together and get that love you need for yourself is to hook your ass up. I am going to say it to again, hook your ass up. Say it to yourself! "I am going to hook my ass up." Now that I think back when I was in my relationship with Rahmel, I wore black (which is still one of my favorite colors) and grey all the time. I still remember how my father would say, "Tee-Tee, why are you always wearing that goddamn black?" Society has taught us to believe that the color black is symbolic for death and you know black people, death scares us. I explained to him that I was not suicidal, I just liked black but now that I'm older I think maybe I wasn't that happy, but that's another story.

Girl, you can do this hook up/Jenny Jones makeover whichever way you want and you can do it for cheap. You really don't have to be rich to hook yourself up. First you have to get some colorful clothes in your life, keep the black for work and those "I feel fat days" but buy yourself something bright like turquoise, pink, yellow, etc. I don't care how dark your ass is, put some color on and make sure you coordinate not match. Coordinate; buy yourself a headband that match with the shirt and I guarantee you, you will begin to feel a little better and begin to like yourself just a little more. Bright colors remind people of their childhood, the days of blow pops and Crayola crayons, so it makes us all very happy. When you walk down the street with these colors on, especially when you have your head up, old ladies will look at you and smile and men would wonder who that little lady is?

Pretty-fying yourself makes you feel good because it puts you in this Barbie doll mode and if you ever saw a Barbie doll, you know they don't look all ugly with a frown on their face. Barbie dolls seem to glow whether they were smiling or putting on that sexy smirk. They exude sexiness and that my friend is something you too should drip of. Sexiness is something that every woman has whether they recognize it or not. I don't care how fat you are or how ugly people say you are, you have something about you that makes you desirable; the hard part is finding that certain something. It's always good to look at yourself in the mirror and try different poses as if you were a contestant on *America's Next Top Model*. The best mirror to use if you want to feel sexy to begin with is the one in the bathroom. I don't know why but for some reason the bathroom is everyone's safe haven away from the world with no judgments. Damn it, if you could pull down your pants and sit your big ass on a toilet and take a dump then you could take thirty seconds to look in the mirror and examine your different looks but you should stay like twenty minutes to get a full observation of your facial features. Doing this will also help you take a better picture of yourself because then you will know which facial expressions work and which ones do not work for you.

I looked at myself in the mirror one day so long that I was almost late for work. I just kept looking and the more I looked the more I discovered how beautiful I actually was. I started to see how much my eyes glowed light brown and how the almond shape of my eyes made room for my high, shiny cheekbones. The more I looked at myself, the more my confidence resurrected. I didn't even notice the bumps on my face caused by a jealous menstruation; I was just caught up in the moment of my sun kissed face.

Now with every pose test and beauty check comes to the main part before checking the body out and that's the teeth check. I know you thought I was going to say hair test, being the weave queen that I am, but no it's the teeth. What I learned is having nice teeth is everything. Yellow or stained teeth are an ultimate no-no and if your teeth is rotten, forget it honey. Were living in the age of Medicaid and there is no excuse for your teeth to look a hot ass mess. What you need to do if your teeth are a little stained or yellow is brush with peroxide, baking soda, and toothpaste.

Once you do that for a couple of weeks you will be set. Buy your self some name brand toothpaste, something like Close Up or Rembrandt, and get the brushing! If your teeth are rotten, you should really invest in some caps or dentures. Teeth are a very touchy topic, believe it or not. Do you want the lady with the red gums with the two sharp, triangular green teeth serving you something like soup at a restaurant? Think about it! That scenario made your stomach hurt a little bit, didn't it? Hell to the no, you don't want her serving your food. Teeth are so important that you can be turned down for a job if your teeth are not correct. You can't sell Real Estate when all someone could think about when you speak is that nasty mouth of yours. Like the booger boy in Elementary School, you will receive your own nickname, like a label branded just to you; something like *Bucky* or my old time favorite, *Yuck Mouf.* When you have messed up teeth, people describe you like that.

We all know a woman who would be popping if she didn't have those messed up teeth. It's like a sin to have bad teeth and it says a lot about you and your hygiene. When people talk about you they go, hey you know this girl named Maria and if they know you they will say who Maria with the messed up teeth? Messed up teeth causes bad breath; and while were talking about the breath thing, people who have bad breath do not care about themselves or the people around you. Getting your mind right means keeping a stick of gum or two in the pocketbook, so ladies get that together and some of you men too because it aint cute, trust me.

The next thing on the list is the hair. Let me tell you a little something about me. I am what we call in the black community, bald headed. My hair, still to this day, never grows past a certain point even in my Jheri curls days. Growing up that was a hard thing to accept probably because I loved doing hair so much and everybody seemed to have long hair. I remember I was the only girl in Kindergarten with extensions in my hair. Don't laugh, I'm serious and it didn't help that my older sister, Toni, was half Puerto Rican with beautiful, long, curly black hair.

Having short hair made me feel alone. Not having long hair really affected my self-esteem until about tenth grade when I realized that I was no longer ashamed to be wearing a weave. Before that having a weave was like a secret. If someone went to touch my head, I would move out the way and I never tried doing styles like putting it up in a bun or something because I was so afraid that my track would show. But now were grown and all styles are now deemed acceptable even Mr. T's mohawk. Wearing pieces is no longer a big deal because were all coming into our own identities. I see girls rocking baldies and ceasars and doing it well like it aint nothing. By the way, I think that short hair is very attractive on women but anyway ladies while doing your little makeover make sure you do your hair.

Please remember that doing your hair will help you out more than you can ever imagine. Hair is what makes the outfit. If you don't have the 'do done, then your outfit is definitely done. I hate when I see chicks with banging outfits then they have one of those scarves (not the flashy/designer ones) covering their heads; it's like what was the point of paying so much for the outfit if you couldn't get your hair done? You dig?

Lastly, in the love yourself department, loving yourself means loving your body. As many old church folk preach to you for years, your body is your temple. Now, I have gone through the most physical appearance stages a female could go through. When I was young, I was underweight. All the boys in both Elementary School and Junior High School did not like me because I was too skinny. My jeans used to not fit my booty like all the other girls and my chest forget about it. Yeah I may be hitting about an E-cup now but back in the days I was the flat chested girl who the boys loved to make fun of because while the girls were rocking training bras, I was still coveting my 3-in-a-pack undershirts with the stars and hearts. It's ok because I went through puberty just in time for the High School.

When High School began I was up to a size 5 in jeans and I was a D-cup. I don't know how that happened, all I know was I prayed like my Aunt Cheryl advised me to do and they grew; so if you want big chest, get the praying or get the paying (plastic surgery). I was my ideal weight, about 135 pounds and ready to take over the world but by the end of high school, 3 years and a cupcake later I was 165 pounds and no longer svelte girl I used to be. I was what they now considered to be really thick (basically one cupcake away from destruction). I was only 5'2 so I wasn't really the bomb anymore. I was too thick for my height and those D's was now DD's and really heavy. I knew I had gained a substantial amount of weight and did not really do anything about it. At that time, I was not going to the gym and I was still getting something to eat outside for breakfast, lunch, and dinner (damn, where did I get all that money from?). I didn't care because, hey, I had my man and I was who I was, and I didn't really care but anything.

Now I am grown and I am definitely a woman with her mind right so I had to step my body game up a notch. So I began to work out and even though I am still really thick, I take care of myself and watch my weight; not for society but for myself. It is important to take care of your body whether you are thick, skinny, or just in between. When you take care of your body, it shows that you love yourself and loving yourself is sexy. I don't know about you but when I see an older lady with a nice body and she has kids, I say to myself, "Wow, that is a bad chick." I appreciate it when I see it because most women don't look like that at her age. Her body, in my opinion, separates her from the rest of the pack and that my dear is what you want to accomplish. And don't let it be a dude with a nice body, hot diggity dog, what could be sexier than that?

A man with a nice body exudes confidence and that my dear is what you need in order to love yourself. Confidence and loving yourself is definitely synonymous with each other. In other words, hit the gym and put down that piece of pie and get ready to love yourself even more because believe me if you are going through something with a man and right now your body is looking so-so and you disappear and come back looking like *Goddamn*, that man is going smack himself because that is intimidating to a weak dude. A cute chick then a cute chick with a nice body (think about it). We have went over the physical things that can make you step your game up and start loving yourself; now lets take a look at the internal. The internal recovery that is needed to get your mind right and love the person who is your skin.

Now that the body is covered, let's get to the soul. You have to let things go in order to clear your conscious and get yourself together. The ability to let go is a great way to step it all up. Letting go anything in the past or present that is bringing you down will definitely make you a little bit happier. Don't let getting your feelings hurt stop you; you got to keep pushing on through the heartache and pain, no matter what someone does to you. Holding around the burdens in your life will only hinder your growth. Like Usher said, "let it burn, when the feeling aint the same in your heart." When Rahmel and I first broke up and he found someone new, I seriously lost my mind. I really started to go a bit crazy by breaking into phone call records, text messages, bank accounts, etc. but when it was time to get myself together I had to let go of the fact that he got with this new chick (so quickly after our breakup) and practically forgot about us. Matter of fact, there wasn't no us, he literally forgot about my ass.

I had to realize that he wasn't my Jesus. I may have made him my all by making him my happiness and my salvation but he wasn't everything that I had in this earth. Realizing this has helped me a whole lot. There are many women out there who make a man their all. They don't care what they do as long as a man in involved and women who live this way will never win in life because what happens when this man disappoint you and leave you high and dry? What are you going to do then?

I also decided to write closure letters to some important men in my life. Rahmel (of course), Jason (the second man in my life that I cared a lot about), and Ali (this guy I used to live next door to that I dealt with occasionally). Writing those letters didn't mean I was never going to talk to them again. It was basically letting them know how I felt because you can't always talk about your true feelings over the phone because second calls interrupt you, or you're screaming trying to explain yourself, or there's a person in the background talking to you. The letters explained to them how I felt in the beginning when I met then, what went wrong, how I presently felt about them, and how I will always feel about them.

One thing about me no matter what I been through and no matter how alone I have been in my early twenties, I have to say that I have met some great men in my life. Almost every man that has come into my life was special for one reason or another. There are people in your life that means something to you no matter what you may say or think. Two of the men that I have wrote closure letters to were extremely special and unforgettable to me. Then there are some people we think we never will forget about but we found out later on that we were completely wrong. I guess we can forget about anyone if we truly wanted to; all we need is a new dude to come along that meet the requirements and we will forget about the past.

I really didn't think about Rahmel when Jason came along and the only time I really thought about him was when Jason was being a bad boy (and that was often). Other than that, no I didn't really think about him. You see we think men get over stuff quickly but were sadly mistaken; they only get over you after they get a new chick to waste time with. Men are weaker mentally than women, however they win in love mostly because they never show all of their true feelings. There wouldn't be so many dead women in the world today if men got over shit so quickly.

They kill these women because they can't believe; well their pride rather, can't believe that she didn't want his ass anymore. It's like it lingers and lingers inside their soul until finally they can't take it anymore then they do something that they could never take back. Now if you break up with a man and sweat him and still treat him like he can always hit it then he won't get crazy. Doing this will only make him feel like he's the winner. You will reap the consequences if a man does not feel like he's the winner in a break up. They are happy if they broke up with you but if you broke up with them and they didn't want it to be over then bang, you're dead. I know this because my Aunt was killed back in 1994 by her child's father.

She broke up with him after being in a relationship for over 11 years; she decided that she could no longer take his drug use, jealousy, and abusive ways. I guess he didn't think that she could get rid of him. He loved her, he adored her beauty, he planted a seed inside of her, and yet he still took her life. He murdered her, so ladies please don't think that things like this don't happen. And don't you try to play them in front of their boys; they will whip your ass quicker than you could blink your eye. That's how men and pride go. I saw a lot of girls get smacked in the middle of the street, in front of everybody just because a man thought she embarrassed him.

Men do not like anyone laughing at them but they don't care if everyone sits there and laugh at you. That's the name of the game, girl. They need a new chick to get by, men front like they could be alone but they really cant. Think about your ex-boo who was too afraid to commit, you got rid of his ass, next thing you know he is committed to the next chick; that's the way love goes.

That's why men sometimes don't like strong women because they like to feel important. If you got a whip, your own crib, and he does not, of course he is going to feel intimidated because he does not feel on top or needed. No matter what men tell you, they want to feel needed. When I used to ask Rahmel for something, especially because I was so independent, he was happy. I don't know if it was because he was generous or was it because he was raised to believe that he was supposed to take care of is woman, all I know is he was always happy to give.

Men like to know that you can't get something unless they give it to you or help you get it. That's why my advice to every woman reading this and even to those who are not: Fuck Niggas, Get Money! I hate to be so mean but if Biggie Smalls could say it to the men, Tionna Smalls could say it to the ladies. Believe me ladies, dick would always be there and being self motivated is the best thing you can possibly be these days.

Having self-reliance is a pure sign of loving yourself. The best thing in the world is to look at something that you want and know some kind of way you can get it. You may can't get it this check but *soon come*. That's what kept me sane after my breakup and even when I had some beef with my parents; I knew I was able to get anything that I wanted.

Were women and even on the plantation in the slavery days, our power was over the Black man's so we can't let him bring us down. Since we were the mistresses of the plantation owner and the domestic caregivers, we were deemed powerful. We were even more powerful than the white women. Don't believe me, go research your history. Anyway some men may not like independent women but you know what, they must respect us. Sadly, most powerful/independent women have a bad attitude but it's only because were tired of these slouch ass men who can't do anything for anybody including themselves, acting up.

Every woman knows a dude that sits there and talks all about money and don't have a pot to piss in and a window to throw it out of. They don't do anything for you because they cant do anything for themselves. All they're really good for is talking. So when you come across a man that feel like they're the man, go ask him a few questions; How are you a Baller and you still sneaking coochie in your Mama's house? How are you a Baller and you're on the bus just like everybody else? Or how you're a Baller and you still sleeping on that broke ass twin bed with the Power Ranger sheets? I guarantee you that these questions will put things in perspective for his ass. He may not call you after you ask him these questions but at least you're letting his ass know that he needs to sit down some-where.

See a lot of times men are being influenced music videos. Many men listen to 50 Cents or Jay-Z and really believe that they are one of them and if he's really delirious, he will believe he's even better than them. We must all remember that we are all the same and were all trying to maintain in this stratified society. What's sad about being an independent woman in the 21st century is we really have no choice but to hold down our own. There aren't many men that we find that are on our level, spiritually, mentally, and financially. Women are the ones now days making them Benjamins and the power moves. Look at Oprah Winfrey, Condeleeza Rice, and even Hillary Clinton, were moving on up. I don't consider myself a Feminist but I do believe in the power of women and definitely the power of a black woman to get over stuff and get their selves right.

Realizing your power is another way to taking control of not only you but your relationship as well. When I was young, I used to curse out my boyfriends in the middle of the street, hey I didn't give a damn, but now I see in any relationship, the woman is in charge and I don't have to show my power by embarrassing the both of us in the streets. Yes, I know you see all these thugged out dudes on the train or even in the mall and it seems like they're so out of control but let me tell you; they play all hard but once their girl or moms say something to them, they calm the hell down.

Some of these so-called thugs that I know, mothers cant even control them, only their woman can. So the next time you want to flip outside, especially if you don't give a damn like me, be quiet and wait to press his ass once you get inside of the house. Now that I am older I realize my power as a woman and now know that being loud doesn't make a person powerful. I am still loud but I have calmed down a whole lot. I have learned now that power comes from practicing what you preach, sticking to your word, and the ability to influence other people around you. Yes ladies, if a man does something like cheat on you, you have no choice but to leave him alone, at least for a while because if you stay with him and he didn't receive any repercussions for his actions, he will not respect you. I said it was over so many times to Jason that after a while he didn't even believe me; I said it so much that after a while I didn't even believe myself, you understand?

I know now that you need to be serious once you say it's over; keep your word, when its over, it's over. Don't play any games with these men. Men love weak women but they will never respect them and that's why you never cry in front of a man; they know they got you so don't even start that crying stuff. Men are like children sometimes, they need a little tough love; they need a woman who is going to stay in his ass if he acts up. People always seem to take kindness for weakness and there is no point of feeling low just for a man. I was born and raised a strong woman, however by the time I broke up with my first love, I began to settle and became nice to these men that I was dating; a mistake at its best. I shouldn't have done that. I became dependent on my next lover for happiness and that's not the way to be. Also, your friends that you hang out with can influence your strength towards certain situation. Hanging out with weak women will, at times, make you weak. I saw how some of my friends let these deadbeat ass dudes play and disrespect them and I guess it sort of rubbed off on me because I was tired of being a bitch. Rahmel made me feel so bad for screaming on him in front of people and always cursing him out that I decided to change and for that I think the next dude tried to run all over me.

Jason never disrespected me as far as curse me out or talk to girls in my face, he just did whatever he wanted to do and did not care about what I did or how I felt about it. I know the strong Tionna Smalls would have left his ass alone a long time ago. But like I said, when you're single, you're always labeled as miserable and my fear to be alone made me want to stay with him. What I realize now is that when you're dealing with somebody and they are not fully on their grind to keep you happy, you're alone anyway. Dealing with him had me thinking that I would never find another guy I liked. See, women must understand that were the leaders of the earth and being strong doesn't make you a bitch, it just makes you informed about life. It makes you understand that if you are not strong; your ass would be taken advantaged of and in the end, hurt.

As a grown ass woman, I don't really believe in being hurt, I believe in being disappointed by men and I'm sure they have disappointed you but I guess we have all disappointed someone in our past. Apart of being a strong woman is admitting your wrong doings, apologizing for it, and then moving on (and never looking back). I don't remember doing many things wrong to the men in my life but I have done some and for that I apologize again because in order to move on with your life, you have to apologize so please apologize to the people that you may have disappointed. Hell, put that in those little closure letters that I advised you to write. In some kind of crazy way I like when someone thinks they are hurting me because it definitely makes me a stronger person and it will definitely do the same thing for you.

When someone thinks you are definitely for them, they will try to hurt you. If someone thinks you're too strong for them they will do stupid little things to bring you down, so my strong Sistas out there be aware! Men get a kick out of messing over a strong woman. I once dated a guy who didn't call me on my birthday knowing that that would hurt my feelings. Ladies, if a man you dealt with doesn't call you on your birthday, he doesn't care about you. Repeat after me: *If* _____ *doesn't call me for my birthday, he doesn't give a damn about me.* Exceptions to the rule are the men in the military who are in the desert and can't give you or his Mama a call. Other than that if he doesn't call, he's a goddamn loser. If he cares he will call you no matter what. If he hates your voice, he should email or even text message you, but the bottom line is he better contact you. There is no excuse for not showing a lady some love on her birthday.

Many things could make you strong. We all have our own gripes out of life and I am not in the position to impose my ideas on you, I am just opening up your brain and helping you think. There is a great question that is good to ask at any hen party, can you stay with a man that cheats on you? I say it all depend on what you think is cheating and basically how long you were involved with the person when I first started dealing with Jason he was still messing with his baby's mother, Shaniqua, who I didn't know anything about. One day after the one-millionth call—a-day she placed to my phone, I decided to meet up with her two hours away in the Bronx and we both confronted his ass. At the time we both thought we were the main girl and I was very convinced that I was the girl for him. So after a long and tired quarrel that ended up getting both of them arrested for fighting in a public place, I was drained.

After Jason was released he admitted that he was still having sex with Shaniqua behind my back. At the time when this event took place we weren't that serious but serious enough where I felt so safe and secure with him and how everybody in my family knew him. So was it cheating? I say no because we weren't labeled as boyfriend and girlfriend and also we just started out but I felt the feeling that a woman feels when she have been cheated on, betrayed, confused; that funny stomach feeling. What pissed me off mostly was the fact that I have asked him plenty of times did he still wants to be with Shaniqua and was he still messing with her. I respect honesty but should have known that he wasn't going to tell the truth, what man would have told the truth in that situation? But then I started taking it as pay back for me still having sex with Rahmel once I knew he had found someone new that he really liked. Ladies and gentlemen,

I want you to know that the old saying is true-karma really is a bitch. In the end all the things you do badly comes back to you and when I look back at this happy but ultra-stupid moment in my life the drama turned me on. Shaniqua may have thought she was making me mad when she kept calling me but for some reason, she was turning me on more to him. I felt this sense of I'm going to win over this bitch like he was the prize but now that I'm wiser I see that he wasn't no prize, he was just the moderator to the bullshit.

He was sexing both of us and loving every moment of it. So no, it wasn't okay when he done that. He placed us both in risk of a Sexually Transmitted Disease (STD). Really, I wasn't the winner and loving yourself is all about being the winner. He was because he got away with messing with her and still had a chance to be with me and inside of my circle of love. Shaniqua had already placed her imprint in Jason's life; she had his child. All I had was hopes and wishes of us to be together, so really who lost? He has been doing her dirty from the beginning of time and yet, she still took him back every time, so another chick he was messing with wasn't a big deal to her. Well, you guys all know who the loser was, it was me. For the first time in my life, Tionna Smalls really felt like a goddamn loser and didn't have the first clue on how to redeem herself.

That situation has showed me that it isn't right for a man to be intimate with another woman unless you both agree to it. You have too much to give and too much to offer to be in a situation like that. That's why now in my life I would prefer to date a man who doesn't have kids because they're Baby Mamas have an affect on these men no matter how much they try to front and I can no longer accept that. Well first of all, that has always been my rule but Jason lied about having kids. Yes, Jason denied his own daughter (how dare he?). Damn, I should have known he was crazy when he did that. I met his daughter later on. She looked like him so much in person that it scared me. I never saw someone that look so much like their father in my whole life.

Seeing his daughter made me see why Shaniqua went so hard and couldn't let him go; she had this little girl who she had to see daily that looked just like him. I understand it now but I refuse to deal with it. I know there are some men out there that are not with their child's mother and they keep it strictly business but I just don't know any. Sorry but you single, childless women deserve a man without the baggage. Kids are a blessing but they are not apart of your reality.

Back in 2006, when my little sister, Bunny, and her husband had a baby, it was beautiful. That was his first child and he (like her) didn't know what to expect. We were all in her hospital room at Jamaica Hospital in Queens and when my nephew came out I looked at my Brother-in-Law's face and he looked like he just hit the lottery. He had the face of a new father: the glow, the promise, and the drive that made this day a special one. His creation was born and there wasn't anything that could take this happy moment away from him. He had to be taught how to hold the baby properly and how not to touch the tip of his head where the brain develops. He had to learn what a father was and that's memories my sister could hold forever in her mind. Now lets say he had another child after my nephew, he would now be experienced. He would know how to do everything so the experience wouldn't be as special. Just like the laws of virginity have taught us, you never forget about your first and my sister was one of the lucky ones to have a man who has never experienced having a child.

Jason and I visited my sister and Brother-in-Law shortly after my nephew was born and I, being the sister who has the least maternal instincts, began to hold my nephew. I thought I looked all cute until Jason screamed, "Boo, hold the baby's head, what are you doing?" I was just like wow, I thought I was holding him correctly but being the *father* that he was, he knew differently or what about the time we came over while my sister was still pregnant and he told her to *eat more greens and have a lot of sex* (it makes it easier for the baby to come out) sounding just like a father. My mother is always the one reminding me of the things that can go wrong later on down the line and she even said out of nowhere, if I ever had a baby from Jason (because I was thinking about my future and things) that I better have a boy because that would be the only thing that really excite him since he already had a daughter. She also said, "He has a kid already, he already been there."

At the time, those words pierced my dreams because I was really opened off of Jason and believed he was the one but now I see that I was very confused. I too began to think that he was too experienced and we wouldn't be sharing the same joys of having a child. The greatest part of life is not knowing. Remember when you thought Santa Claus was real and we closed our eyes during a sex scene in a movie, inexperienced. Shaniqua probably ended up being the winner. Having his baby when he was young (17 years-old) and scared and trying to find out what it was like to have a child; knowing him he probably asked every man what they felt when they had a kid. *Puuuuulease!!!* You deserve to be the first. A man with a child life revolves around that child and its mother.

You can't compete with his child's mother because she will always share a special bond with him. All his attention should be on you and your child. You should not have to share the limelight. Sounds a little mean, but oh well. Don't get me wrong I know there are some men out there that is are excited about the birth of all their kids but I say it's not the feeling, it's the drama free life your ass would have if your man don't have any kids. Imagine this: Your guy of a year has a daughter from a previous relationship. You have never met his daughter before because his daughter's mother is mad that he has moved on and said, "I don't want a new chick around my kid. " So out of respect for her, he keeps his daughter away from you. How could the relationship evolve without you meeting the other half of him? Or what happens during birthday parties and graduations? Is he supposed to leave you in the house to be with his "family"? I think not. If you do have a guy that doesn't care what his Baby Mama says then good for you but for others ask yourself this, Is it loyalty between the two or is there still hope they'll reconcile and they don't want to confuse the child? I say if you have so much loyalty to your Baby Mama then you might as well be with her.

And you Baby Mamas out there, yeah you, stop keeping the men away from their kids just because they don't want to deal with you in a relationship sense. All you're doing is making it worse for your child because every child should know their father and stop trying to keep the new chick away because you know when you get a new man that wants to be involved with you and your kid, you will have them by your child. I'm not saying allow anyone by your kids but remember these men are going to do whatever they want regardless and you can't stop anyone from doing what they want to do.

Some men like to play the Baby Mama card against you childless woman but you know what, don't worry about it. You're better off without the kid. I once too was jealous of a man's kid but then when I thought about it, I am better off than the Baby Mama because while she is sitting home with a crying ass kid, I have the benefit of going asleep peacefully without the aggravation, thanks. Also when a man decides one day that I am not the woman for him, I don't have a kid that I have to look at everyday that reminds me of him and that steamy night. Please understand ladies that aint nothing change but the game and if a man aint shit before the kid, he definitely wont be shit after the kid, so don't have a baby for him, have one for yourself because if he ever decides to leave, that child will always be your responsibility. I, myself don't have children because I have never met anyone I felt so excited about that I wanted to reproduce with.

Over the years, I thought about children but I guess I still don't see it as a reality, maybe it's because I am still very young. I love my niece and nephews but everyone isn't maternal and please don't feel bad if you are like myself and are not into children. It is time for women to stop conforming to society. Why is it if a woman does not have kids by 30-years-old in the black community, she is looked upon as being infertile? I truly believe that children are a blessing but they aint always a good thing if you are broke. See, so there isn't anything wrong with waiting until you are financially stabled to start your family. Don't get me wrong I am not a abortion supporter but I do believe that your ass should choose to have children when you're prepared mentally, physically and financially because there is not anything worse than a dirty ass kid.

A dirty ass kid is the kid you see in the street with tore up sneakers on (and they are white, for some reason they always have light sneakers on), the kid that looks like he hasn't had a haircut in months, and their clothes are often wrinkled and unmatched. It's the kid you see on the train that appearance makes you shake your head and say, "now his mother knows she need her ass whip." You could tell that this kid is unsupervised when he leaves the house in the morning and he is not receiving the proper attention or financial support that he deserves from his parents. I personally hate when I see this. It's like something in my heart cries for this mess. Note to all the mothers out there: If you are broke with one kid, please protect yourself and don't have another one! Because when a child is considered the *bum* of the class it really messes them up psychologically.

I once met a man named Karl who was raised in South Jamaica, Queens. I thought Karl was very attractive, he was tall (just like I like 'em) and he had swagger for days. Anyway, we started sharing childhood stories and he stated that he grew up poor and I just disregarded what he said and kept on yapping my mouth. As weeks went by I noticed that this dude was a cheap ass bastard. Then I realized that he kept mentioning his misfortune he had as a child and sadly I really couldn't relate because as a child I was kind of spoiled. In Public and Junior High School I didn't have everything I wanted but I damn sure I had everything I needed, thanks to my parents. And even when I did want to front like I was ultra fly I wore one of my older sister's Donna Karan shirts that my Grandmother (God bless her soul) bought for her.

So honestly, I didn't understand his situation too much but I did go through other things growing up as a child and although it affected me, I didn't mention everyday. Karl would often tell me stories that would make me mad like how he was the only kid coming back from Christmas break with the same sneakers on his feet that he left with and how while kids played with their new Nintendo Game Boys, he had only a jigsaw puzzle of the world globe from the nearby convenient store (I guess that's why he could point out any country on the map without a single thought). It sickened me to know that one of his toes never grew to its full potential because he kept wearing sneakers 2 sizes too small because those the only ones his next door neighbor, Sonny, had to lend him. Are you getting my point?

Growing up like this has changed Karl's life as a man and although he was grown now and making over $40,000 a year while living with minimal bills, he still lived his life as if he was a poverty stricken person. He often chose to eat peanut butter and jelly sandwiches for dinner over buying him a meal from the Chinese restaurant. So parents if you have to have 3 jobs to take care home, please do so. Hell S.S.S (Sell Some Socks) because kids did not ask to be here. I know that times are hard but it wouldn't be as hard if we saved up more money and stop trying to make sure our children have every pair of Jordan's (especially since Michael Jordan could care less about the black community. Hell, he rides by the same community in his Bentley where kids kill each other everyday over a pair of his over priced sneakers) and make sure we save for the future incase you do lose your job after being there for more than ten years.

The greatest thing, well one of the greatest things about being a woman is the act of preparation. A woman can prepare herself for almost anything I don't care what it is. So ladies, my best advice that you would find in this book is: In life, be prepared for disappointments. When meeting a man, I am not saying think the worse, I am simply saying imagine the worse so when he does do some crazy-off-the-wall shit, y face so I wasn't as upset when I came over his house to do his mom's (Lisa) hair and he had Shaniqua's picture placed up in his room on the wall. The picture looked like it has been crumbled and ripped previously but was obviously placed on the wall once he found out I was coming over to do his mom's hair.

You see men always try to hurt your feelings and I was about to flip until his brother Jaleel, convinced me to calm down and not make a fool of myself and then I also prepared myself for this day when he would flaunt the fact that he was back with Shaniqua in my face. I was kind of disappointed but then I thought it was better that she was with his trifling ass than me because in reality he was a dog and he was never going to change. Whenever a man thinks he hurt you by going back to a bad situation, huff, puff, cry in the shower, and then get over it because it's truly his loss and his stupidity.

Losing It All in the Name of Love

We all say those three little words: I love you. That four-letter word, love, seems so important when you're in a relationship. It's like something in our soul beast to hear those words whether the person saying it means it or not. We all like to say the word but have we ever thought about what the word love actually means. I surveyed many people about this word and the answers were all the same. Love is sacrifice; love is commitment; love is doing things you wouldn't normally do; love is giving your all. Those are the definitions of love that we were all raised on but in reality there is no true meaning of the word love, just interpretations of it.

We all were raised to believe that when you had a different feeling for someone or when you felt like you couldn't be with out that person, you loved them. As children, our parents said they loved us when we left the house and as adults, our mates told us they loved us after a certain point in the relationship. It's like there's something wrong with your man if he didn't say he loved you after being in a relationship with you for more than 6 months. We sit and look for that word for validation that the relationship is going great. The word love has been turned into a social construct; you have to say the word love if you want to be labeled as normal.

What I have discovered in myself and in other women is that the word love is what controls the whole relationship. Many women prey on hearing that four letter word and if their man miss a day of saying it, they feel distraught. What we don't realize is men, many of the times; use the word just to mess up your mind. They know that if they want something from you they have to pretend like they love you and care about you over the next chick. Its like the word love doesn't mean shit anymore, its just one big game. If the word meant great regard, sacrifice, and deep care for another, why can't we say any word in replace of it? For an example, instead of saying "I love you," why can't I say, "I adore you." Why can't I replace the word love with fish, or hump, or dance? I can't replace it with those words because of the norms that were placed in the world. Society has taught us that *love* was the only word we can use to express how we feel. That's the only word people say and that's the only word people want to hear.

We don't realize that the word was something that was made so people could do anything wrong to you. For example, how many times do you hear yourself or other women around you say, "I know he loves me, but." What is the word *but* about? When someone says this they are making an excuse. It's like a man can do whatever he wants as long as he says he loves you. Are you kidding me? I also hear this word a lot when the ladies and I sit around and talk about men cheating on women. Grown ass women sit and say that *Baby Boy* shit, "He loves me and he just screws that chick." It's sad how we allow the word love to monopolize our whole life. What we don't understand is that the media influence our perception of love. Doesn't it make you creamy when you see a man on television tell his woman he loves her? It's like the word love is some sort of tool of psychology meaning the strongest woman in the world could fall victim of the word.

Losing it all in the name of love is like being a sucker for love. A sucker for love is a person who would do anything just to feel loved. A type of woman who doesn't care about anything or anybody if her man is acting right that week. People who suffer from the sucker for love disease are really pitiful; they would sell their own mother out just for a man's affection. It doesn't matter what the man does, like a sucker, she's back up smiling in his face waiting for him to pat her on her ass. The sad thing is this type of individual doesn't believe that they are as sprung as they really are. They're not even sprung over the man; they're sprung over the word love. They need to hear the word, they need to feel the word, and most of all they need to say the word.

Sucker for loves are the worse people you can come across because they would do anything to feel that way including fucking your man. It's like as long as someone love them they are okay. Don't get me wrong, we all want to feel loved but why fall victim to the bullshit, knowing that a man doesn't love you if he disrespects you by cheating or hitting on you. People who are obsessed with the word love settle many times in their relationship because they are afraid that their man wouldn't love them anymore if they spoke up for themselves. The women who I know that are suckers for love settle on a man not making her his priority; they settle on a man not giving them anything (his affection or his cash), and they accept being a back burner bitch.

Women like this lose it all for a man; their morals, their goals, and their say in a relationship. All a man has to say is they love her and she jump up and do whatever it is that he wants. What I am saying in this chapter is it's time for us to stop getting stupid because a man says he loves us because it's bullshit half of the times anyway when a man says it. Most men say they love a woman in the average of three months and vice versa but how could you truly love someone in that short of a time? You barely know a person in three months much less care enough for them that you are willing to sacrifice it all for them. It takes about a year to get to know someone, so don't get mad if a man does wait that long to tell you that; at least he waited to say it when he felt he really meant it.

What I have come to realize in my post-relationship life is women who say that word less are the winners in relationships. Its like men expect you to say this word after dealing with them for a while because many women do but trick his ass and try your best not to say it even if you do mean it until you feel that the feelings are mutual. There is nothing worse than telling a man who doesn't have a bone in his body that cares about you that you love him. The sad thing is the man would most likely say it back to you even though he doesn't feel the same way because he's afraid to hurt your feelings because he's not thinking anything of it. I say don't say it first also because it will show him that you are not like most women he know who be beasting to hear that word. It shows him that you are a girl who doesn't have your feelings on your sleeve and that you are weighing every situation that you come across with your mind and not your heart.

It's like there are invisible responsibilities and rules that comes into a relationship once that word is said. I believe that love is a technical word that changes the makeup of a relationship. Sean, one of the people who I surveyed for this chapter, said it best, "Females are too emotional. When I say I love you that mean to me that I care or I'm there for you and I really like you. That doesn't mean I want to be with you or I am in love." He later on uses the example, "Lets say we talk everyday for 5 months and its getting somewhere and I say 'I love you' and you feel that I am serious everything is gonna change especially the way you look at me." See, that example shows that men are aware of how the word love changes things in a relationship.

The bad thing about feelings is that most of the time we confuse the word love for infatuation. You could dig a person's style, enjoy being around them, and making love to them that doesn't mean you love them; you could just be infatuated over that person or better yet, lusting over that person. Love doesn't give up just because something goes wrong or because your feelings are hurt. As I write this chapter, I look back at the men that I said I love you to. I never was a lovey-dovey type of girl but still I said I love you to a few and now I am realizing that most of the men I could have sworn I loved, I loved them in a friendship way. Take my friend Ali, the cockiest man in Brooklyn who I met as a young Brooklyn child running wild. I have been obsessed for years thinking that I loved him but in reality, I don't love him. I was just amazed by his attitude and loved figuring him out and picking his brain.

I take a look at my best friend Perry, who I knew since 7th grade. I love him meaning I would do anything for him but I love him more as a friend, not as someone I would drop it all for but he's someone with a little more time, I could grow to love and love forever. My second boyfriend, Jason, is another person who I loved more as a friend now that I am thinking about it. That was the man who I lusted after; I have never felt the feeling of lust before I met him and that is what that's about it. When I think about it, the only man I loved was my first love Rahmel. I still love him but not in that sort of way but that's the only man I loved in a relationship sort of way and that's why now I am taking my time with other men and making sure I don't tell them something that I don't mean.

When you're young and you're dealing with a man, you think you love everybody but you don't. We have to remember that there are so many different kinds of love that you can have for a person; you can love them as a friend, a brother, a cousin, a confidant, a father, etc. Don't close your mind up to just one feeling; explore your emotions with each different person so you can know where everyone stands in your life.

You should never become a victim of love, whether you love the person or not. Love is something that is supposed to uplift your relationship-not bring it down. You are the problem if you have to hear the word love to believe someone cares greatly about you and plan on doing you right. Its time for us to ask ourselves, are we truly in love or infatuated with a person? One thing we all can agree on is that it takes maturity to really love someone and also we can't love anyone until we love ourselves. So ladies, let's stop falling victim and take back our lives and our emotions, better yet, lets stop saying the word in general until we are 100% sure we really mean it.

Jealousy & Envy

✦

Jealousy won't get you nowhere—Anonymous

The person who invented the quote, "It's lonely on your way to the top," was a genius. This is one of the most important things that you must remember while reading this book. Reading this book will definitely open up your mind to things you haven't thought about in a while. I know this because it had the same affect on me and I am the one who wrote this book. I must tell you that I have lost a lot of friends and men while writing this book.

One day as I was sitting in my bedroom thinking about my future, I realized that I didn't want to die a nobody. A nobody meaning a person who hasn't left their mark in the world and achieved greatness; achieved something that most people have not. All my life I dreamed of doing the unthinkable and call it what you want, I never doubted myself and I always knew that one day all of my dreams would come true. One problem that I have even until this day is I share my plans with too many people. I mean I share my plans with members of my family, my friends, my men, and even strangers. My mother always tells me to stop telling people my plans because everybody is not going to be happy for me but I never listened. She used to make me mad whenever she would say this but

I am starting to see what she is saying now that I am beginning to move on up in the world.

The first thing you lose while you're on your way to the top is your friends. Yes, those same females you stayed up all night and talked out your dreams and your problems with. When you get excited about something that you want to do, the first person you always seem to tell is your best friend. If you are the kind of person (like so many people) that always come up with bright ideas but never go through with them, your friends wont begin to hate on you but if you are the type of gal that does everything she says she is going to do then you are in for a huge surprise once you finally do try to achieve your dream. I found out that what my mother has always told me was right, your friends isn't interested in every dream that you may have. The best thing for you to do when you are trying to achieve something is to stop talking and remember that actions speak way louder than words. When you shut your mouth and act out your dream, they will start to believe you and that's what I did when I went about writing this book.

In the beginning, most of my friends encouraged me to write this book; I guess it was that they were tired of hearing my mouth. It was all good until they finally saw that I was taking this book writing thing seriously. All of a sudden every time they heard from me I was talking about my book that was supposed to change the way females thought about love and life. I think the more serious I became about my *Get Your Mind Right* campaign, the more I began to write and the more I wrote, the more I talked about certain issues that I was going to discuss in the book.

Writing this book started out as a girls-talking-shit manuscript then I began to realize that this book was going to reach readers all across the country who are in need of some real empowerment. At that point, I began to take my responsibility as a message sender very seriously. Every conversation I had with women, no matter what age they were, I wrote something from it. I could be on the train, in school, in church, wherever, I was writing. That's when I discovered that women from all walks of life were experiencing the same problems: Men and the lack of self-esteem.

Writing this book has opened up my eyes to many situations that were lingering around me; situations that were always right under my nose. The more I wrote, the more I saw how trifling men were and how weak women were for them. I didn't have this attitude coming into the book but it snuck up on me. Before writing this book, I thought just girls who didn't have anything were the only ones obsessed with the deadbeat dudes. I thought it was only the uneducated that sacrificed it all for love but you know what I was wrong. I too began to realize that I was a guilty of losing it all for love. I too was obsessed with hearing those four letter words so much that I often called my ex-boyfriend just so that he could end the conversation with, "I love you." I was unstoppable once I found out this about myself and as I grew stronger, I tried to make my friends even stronger.

I would tell my friends little things that I have learned about the makeup of a woman's emotions and why we wanted love and why we felt we needed love solely from the person we felt we loved. All of my so-called friends were down with me when I first began this search for self-love and respect. They looked to me as the motivator, they told me their hardships and I told them mine. What you will realize once you are self-sufficient is that you are never afraid to tell your story because everyone has a testimony. That's apart of being grown, being able to tell your story to a friend, a little girl who may look up to you, or even your mate without feeling embarrassed or ashamed.

The first time I realized I was growing into a self-loving coon is when I admitted to my friends that the guy I was seeing at the time did not like me for me any longer and tried to play me with sleeping with his child's mother. When I told some of my friends this with a serious face, they looked at me in shock. See, in order to get yourself together, you have to keep it real to yourself and everyone around you. Admitting the faults in my love affair helped me get myself together. It took a couple of months but I changed myself from an attention-loving-affection needed person into a calm, cool, and collective person with the men. I no longer felt I needed a man; I became so reliant on myself for happiness that it was ridiculous.

Life began to really feel different to me. I told my friends every day how I felt about life and I think they started to see my growth as I became reluctant to talk to them about their never-do-right dudes. I could hear their sob stories all night before I started getting my stuff together and writing this book but as time went on, I began to get sickened by their "my man has some chick texting him" or "he went missing in action for the whole weekend" stories. I stopped looking down on the men and began to look at my friends. Yes my friends: young, black, educated, driven women who had the whole world in their hands and still letting these deadbeat guys who shouldn't have smelled the cooch in the first place, play them. I couldn't help getting sick after a conversation that ended off with, "Oh, he played himself." I was becoming smart enough to know that the guy didn't play himself-he played her.

I told my friends about my new revelation about life hoping that that would stop them from trying to hurt my soul with their stories that really had a simple answer: Get rid of him! But they kept telling me their stories. I believe that if you are a true friend, you will tell your girl when she's slipping. One thing that I, Tionna Tee Smalls, hate is when a girl continuously gets played by a man; they're what I call professional victims-they are used to getting played. Don't get me wrong everybody plays the fool (sometimes) but damn, how many times are you going to let the same dude play you? Men play women and women play men; it's all apart of the game we play called life. See, what most women don't understand is, it's not about getting played; it's about what you do after you get played. No matter what anyone tells you, if someone plays you once, its shame on them but somebody plays you twice, its shame on you. If you sit there and continuously let your man disrespect you and treat you like he doesn't care if you stayed or left, then you are the fool. Respect means more than love and twice as important than sex in any relationship.

Why wouldn't someone take advantage of a person they know they could do whatever to and get away with it? I honestly told my friends this in good faith, thinking that this would make them tired of the bullcrap just like I was but I was wrong. My low tolerance for wackness didn't give me kudos from my friends it caused resentment from them. One in particular, who we won't name, started to hate telling me anything about her low-life man. I understand that because if she would have told me some slouch ass story about her man, I would have shut her down but she stopped speaking to me on casual terms as well. I don't know, maybe her man tricked her into thinking that I was the enemy that wanted them to be apart but he was sadly mistaken if he thought that because one thing about me is I want people who are happy to be together. I love seeing two beautiful people who are happy, healthy, and free being together; seeing that gives me hope for the world.

So my friend and I got into a big spat about her man because I approached her about her choice about cutting our friendship because I really liked her as a friend and didn't want this *Mind Wrecker* (see introduction for more on those types of men) to get in between our friendship. I guess it's true what Mama always said, "Never tell a female about her man," but oh well. True friends don't let other friends get bamboozled by lame dudes so I told her how I felt.

My advice is if someone did something that bothered you, speak up, and don't wait until tomorrow when it blows up to get if off of your chest. Our friendship basically ended from that day forward. We were talking about one thing (her man) and then in a split second, the conversation went all wrong when she insulted me about something negative that I have been dealing within myself. Now here's the rule to friendship, no matter what when you argue with your friends (because you are going to argue with them, they're like your sisters), you never get personal. Let's say you and your friend is arguing about whether pancakes and grits match for breakfast, you don't tell her she's a nasty fat bitch because she told you that you don't know what you're talking about; you understand me? Being a nasty fat bitch doesn't have anything to do with pancakes and grits, maybe being fat has something to do with it but the insult is not necessary for your already heated debate. Nonetheless, the insult started a big thing in our clique of friends. While we were having this argument, she said, "You hate men because of the *little* book you're writing." That brings me to the topic of this chapter, jealousy.

When someone refers to something you do as little, they are taking a stab at your integrity. We all have a friend who says, "Oh, her little apartment is nice," or "That's a nice little car." When the word *little* is used to describe something, the person intent is to hate. I had to explain to her first and foremost that I wasn't a man hater, just a woman who hated slouch dudes who thought that they were the best thing to a black woman since the straightening comb. Secondly, I had to explain to her that there wasn't anything that I have ever done that could be considered as little. See that right there was supposed to make me feel like I wasn't good enough to write a book or my book wasn't going to have as much success but it didn't because having a clear mind has prepared me for the hate that was coming my way.

Now this was coming from a girl who had a lot going on for herself (good looking, nice car, nice job, etc.) and looks what happened? It doesn't matter what a woman has going on for herself, if she doesn't love herself and have confidence, she will be a hater regardless. Believe it or not, people become jealous of you for the most tedious reasons; I know people who are jealous of me because I speak up for myself or because I wear bright colors. I came to the realization that hate has no face.

I thought that jealousy amongst friends only happened with the young (30-and-under) crowd but I was sadly mistaken. My mother has friends who are jealous of her also. I am talking about women who are married and making just as much money as she does, jealous for no reason. I used to always watch my mother's friends and would notice that every time they were around my parents with their man, they would kiss on purpose to show my parents that they too were in love. That is basically a sign of a person who is jealous of her relationship. There were also times that my mother would talk about the amount of time she has been on her job and her friends would try to out do by telling her some bogus story about them being on their job even longer. I used to bug out when I witnessed this because it was truly funny to me.

Whether you're young or old, there are surefire ways to tell if someone in your team is jealous of you. The first sign is friends who compete with you. Oh boy, that's the worse type of hater; please believe me! I used to have this friend named Destiny who I went to go to college with. Destiny was very pretty; she was tall and brown skinned with pretty long black hair. She was the kind of girl who you would imagine getting all the attention if you bring her around men. She was out of sight but she was missing that swagger (swagger and confidence is essential to have as a woman). She was smart and good looking but at times she was a little corny. She was the type of girl who you would think had it all together but didn't. She was an undercover hater who hung out with females who never did anything with themselves; in other words, she liked to hang out with deadbeats who didn't look or dress as well as she did so she could get all of the attention.

Then she started hanging out with me and my crew. The crew of sexy women of all shapes and flavors who were doing what they had to do to get that paper. Destiny was the type of girl who had a video girl body but never made much use of it when she bought clothes that didn't compliment her frame. I, on the other hand, was all into buying whatever showed the cup of the tittees and the tightness of the booty so I always got my attention when I was around her. She never shopped with us but every time we bought something, she would be like, "Where did you get that from?" or "How much did you pay for it?" I don't care where you got it from or how much you paid for it; you got beat in your head (according to her). No matter what new item you bought, she already been up on it years ago and you were just catching up. I mean, she was the type of girl who had a lot of designer shit but was often labeled as a *Has-been* because she always talked about how fly she was in the good old High School days. She didn't realize that she still had it going on but often looked stupid because she claimed to be fly yet she rocked the same designer pocketbooks over and over. It was like her way of showing you she had it. And she wouldn't only compete with you over the finer things that chicks would kill for; she would compete with you for men too.

No matter how cute you think you may be, there is someone out there in the world who is cuter than you. According to her, every man who tried to talk to us over her was corny. She didn't understand that every man wasn't going to be attracted to her even though she could easily be mistaken for a top model; her attitude was like if a man didn't like her something was wrong with him and don't let it be a guy we all knew trying to diss her; it would be, "Oh he used to sweat me." She was just real sickening. She didn't understand that we were all friends, living in the same freaked up world and that sometimes you're going to win, but at other times, you are going to lose. She didn't understand that it wasn't cute to compete with her friends. We were supposed to do it big together, not go against each other. That's a code one must abide in order to be in a clique of friends.

Anyway, the second clue of a hater is when your friend never compliments you. You have one friend that no matter what you do or what you wear, she never gives you your props; it's like it kills her to give you a compliment. You know you look good by her facial expressions and gestures but she will never tell you. A person who does this to you is trying to break down your self-esteem because they don't have any of their own. If you have one of these in your crew, stay far away from this person. This is the type of person who would see a booger in your eye and won't tell you because she doesn't want you to be the cute one.

The funny thing about this kind of a hater is she's cute too. That's the most sickening problem of this kind of hater, she's cute too but like Destiny, she wants to be the only cute one. She doesn't want any competition around, she just wants to be the star and she believes by not complimenting you, you will start to feel a little insecure about yourself. And sometimes when you have friends that do to this you, you start to question yourself a little bit but don't fall into the bullcrap, you're just experiencing that little something called hate. With this kind of hater, the best cure for them is for you to just always stay true to your style and keep looking good.

The last sign of a jealous person is when you are telling a friend of yours your plans for the future and all she has to say is, "umph." That is one gesture that was created from the devil to destroy you. A real friend would have a lot to say regarding your future endeavors and would never try to downplay your goals and dreams. Your real friend would not discourage you by making sound affects and being quiet. I have plenty of ex-friends that used to do this to me and I know what time it is when I hear this expression. Watch out when you experience this because the person you think is your friend may just be another critic waiting for your downfall so that they could give the rest of the world a bad review of your performance.

Now we're going to get to the type of jealousy and envy they won't teach you about in school-the jealousy from your man. When you hear the word jealousy and man put together, you automatically think of a person who won't let you go out to the clubs or talk to other men because he is afraid of losing you. Well that's a type of jealousy but that's one that's not really valuable enough to document in *Girl, Get Your Mind Right!* It would be healthy for you to get away from those types of assholes as well but were talking about the loser who is jealous of his own woman's success and the attention she receives from others. I like to call this the *My Wife is an Actress Syndrome* based on a European movie whereas a well to do man is jealous of his wife's career as a professional actress.

The woman is the center of attention everywhere the couple goes and he grows jealous and envious of her throughout the whole movie. Maybe you can't relate to this movie but I have another example of a jealous man, which is in R&B singer Ashanti's *Rain on Me* video. When the video first start you see a clip of Ashanti (playing herself) and her boyfriend Andre (played by Lorenz Tate) arguing about him not being able to see her as often as he would have liked. "It's like you have to fit me into your busy schedule," he exclaims to Ashanti during the argument in which she is pleading to him that that's not the case at all, she was busy with her singing career. You see these two fighting and going at it the whole time in the video. There's a scene in the video in which Ashanti and Andre is in the car getting some food from a drive thru restaurant. They get their food and Ashanti face is plastered on the cup of large sodas.

The face he makes when he sees this is priceless; he made one of those *not this bitch again* faces (funny stuff).

They had a lot of sexual chemistry because no matter how many times he knocked her ass out, she stayed and made passionate love to him. Maybe that *Baby Boy* stuff turns you on but for me, it was just sickening and proving how much stuff a deadbeat ass man could get away with if he tried. As you can tell from the so-called drug transaction in the video, Andre was a Street Pharmacist who drove the expensive car Ashanti bought him with her hard earned money. He complained about her making money yet he didn't have a problem spending her money; that's a deadbeat for you (and I will say this if it was a woman doing this to a man). He had a famous girlfriend yet he still needed to dip into the street life. He had nerve to smoke a blunt while looking at the billboard of Ashanti; if that's not jealousy, I don't know what is.

Now there are two versions of this video, the one you saw on *BET* or *MTV* and the extended version (that was too hot for T.V.) where as the girl who Andre was caught with asked him "Is that Ashanti?" when Ashanti walked in and caught them on top of each other. Ashanti told him the relationship was over and to get his stuff and get out and his reply was, "Stop, I love you." Bottom line was he left after the fight and got into his car and started to think about the argument they had gotten into. He ran the red light just thinking of the pain, stopped, and a big ass tractor-trailer truck hit him. The car was totaled and Andre was killed in the car accident. It is unclear whether or not Andre killed himself by stopping in the middle of the road but the main point is he was extremely jealous of the woman he was being intimate with.

I know it was just a video but it had a lot of realism in it. Videos are apart of art and art is apart of reality. He cheated on her to make her feel low and got himself in a car accident just so that she could feel like it was all her fault for breaking up with him in the first place. This is something that goes down in relationships all the time. Sure you may not be Ashanti, a platinum recording artist, but you are a beautiful hardworking woman out to get yours and some men can't handle it. When your man sits and acts like he's mad at you whenever you accomplish a big goal, he is a hater no matter how you may look at it. When he questions why you bought yourself a new bag or a new dress and don't pay any of your bills, he's a hater. When he doesn't tell people about your achievements, he's a hater. I had a friend whose boyfriend didn't even tell his mother that she had graduated from college-Haha! Funny stuff. He was definitely a hater.

The worse thing that can happen to you is your man being jealous of you. As I spoke about in the introduction of this book, a person who is jealous of you will bring you down eventually. I once was in love with a hater and he tried everything in his power to bring me down. He used to look at me as competition. He used to see me with new things and make faces. I really couldn't believe it. Always remember a person who is jealous of you is liable to could kill you. Make sure if you a strong woman, you get yourself a strong man who would complement your life and not burden you with his own insecurities. The cure for a jealous man is to never dwell on your faults around them because men prey on your bad points. It's not good to say, "Oh, look how fat my stomach is," because then he knows that that bothers you and will throw it in your face later on. Don't give these dudes no bait; keep your insecurities to yourself!

The problem with many women is they look into their man (who they don't know is a hater) for the stamp of approval regarding their looks. It's nice when they give it to you but that stamp would be the same stamp that they will throw in your face when they tell you how fat, dirty, or stink your pussy is and that goes for friends as well. So, remember ladies, telling your business and looking for gratification from your lover and friends is never a good way to go. All it does is give them something to talk about when they decide to destroy your ass later on.

The sad thing about most jealous people is they don't realize that they are haters. They really don't see the things that they are doing to other people. And at times, we don't think they are haters either but I came up with something called, *Hater Language.* Hater Language is things jealous people say to demean other people and uplift their own egos. Here are three examples of how haters say one thing but mean another thing:

1.   The hater would say something like: *She has a nice little house*
     What the hater meant to say is: She's doing big things by buying that house.

2.   The hater would say something like: *What you need to do* (regarding a situation you may be in)
     What the hater meant to say is: She doesn't have a clue to what you need to do but want to say anything to get you off your game.

3.   The hater would say something like: *What do you need a new one for?* (When you're buying a car or a new dress)
     What the hater meant to say is: Damn, she stays buying new stuff.

Those are just examples but we all know people that talk like this and they don't even recognize the hate they have within themselves. Be careful around these haters and make sure your ears stay alert and when you witness the hate, handle your business and cut them right off. Watch their actions, their words, their movements, and I guarantee you that you will be able to recognize a snake faster than you would have if you sat there and ran your mouth. People always think they are slick, so don't let them know that you see what they are trying to do. Just let them try to strike so that they could fall on their face when they are trying to cause you harm.

You should also watch the haters who always have something to say about something that is going on in your life. What you need to remember is, opinions are like assholes, and everyone has one so never be stressed out by what someone else says about you. People are going to talk about you regardless; hell, they talked about Jesus.

In the end, a hater is always a person you should get rid of in your life. You can't help it, if you are cute or if you have a nice butt (hey, she needs to blame God or your Mama, not you). There is never a reason to be envious of another human being because whatever it is that person has you can get with a little determination. But I guess in the end, haters are needed in the world because when they stop hating that's when you know that you are getting off of your game. Keep the haters talking and you, my friend get the walking. Never stress the haters and stay focus and remember jealousy and envy comes with the territory when you're a bad chick.

Cheating

A question that many young women asked me while I was writing this book was, why do men cheat? When asked this I thought to myself, why the hell do I know? What I started to see was this was not only young girl's asking this but grown ass woman as well. So I sat in my lab (my bedroom) and begin to research why do men cheat? My first avenue of finding this answer for you guys were by interviewing guys on the topic of cheating. So I went online to Myspace and posted the question. At the time I had over 1500 friends, so I thought that this was the perfect way to survey a lot of men at one time for no money. The answers I received really intrigued me not only as a woman but as an intellect as well.

First off, let's clear up a lot of myths that you may have about cheating. Not only fat and ugly girls get cheated on; men cheat on pretty girls too and the sad thing is they cheat with uglier women. Hell, look at Halle Berry. Secondly, it doesn't matter if you do everything sexually for your man, if he's a dog and he wants to cheat, he will do it anyway. Now I have a few theories when it comes down to cheating and I know that some of you are going to read this and think that I am totally out of my mind. For one, when you're dating, there's no such thing as cheating. So what you have a guy that you mostly see, you are allowed to date and make love to anyone that want as long as it's safe and consensual. Many women and some men feel that when you're dating them that seeing another person on the side is off limits. I think that's a whole crock of shit by the way. Dating is not definitive; dating is like tasting the sample before you decide to buy (which is marriage). Now if you're in a relationship (meaning you two guys dated and now you've both made the adult decision to be committed to one another) that's another story and I still say that that's not your husband so he still doesn't have any handcuffs on the booty, you feel me?

As you all know, communication is important to any relationship. You should have the talk before you two become exclusive in a relationship. In case you don't know what the talk is, the talk is laying down the rules and regulations of the relationship. That's the time when you and your mate discuss what is cheating to one another. Cheating is different to different people. To you, cheating may be your man having a conversation with the opposite sex on the phone or flirting with that Receptionist at his job. To him, cheating may be you still having a friendship with your ex or just plain making friends with guys you meet on the train. See, you won't know how your man view things until you have that talk. Some people believe that even your thoughts can be considered as cheating but I say if that's the case, were all some cheaters and going straight to hell on a stick.

I think apart of getting your mind right and being a woman overall is being able to be in touch with reality. Now what is reality? Well, in reality almost everybody cheats whether they think so or not. There are a lot of people in the world and it's hard to be happy with just one. I often joke to friends that I need two boyfriends, one could be what I call my Christmas (the dude that makes me go crazy sexually) and one could be my comfort (the man I grow old with who has the stability that I need to survive) because it is very hard to find both. If you find a man that spends all dough on you and treat you like a Queen, his pipe game sucks. If his sex is official, then he's broke. It's like you can't find a man who has it all and if you did find one, kudos to you, keep his ass. We feel like this and were women so you can imagine how a man may feel.

I know we like to act all innocent but let's face it ladies, sometimes were bigger whores than men. Some of the best cheaters I have come across have been women. They cheat hard bodied and their man doesn't even have a clue. Women are better cheaters than men because were better liars than men. Men get caught up in their double lifestyle because they get sloppy while doing their dirt. The best thing about when women cheat is if we cheat, there's a reason for it; with men, they cheat just to cheat. Most of the times men are not needy for another woman, they're just greedy.

See when we go dip out on our mate and have sex with that new guy at the job, we plot our steps very carefully. We know when were going to give him (lets say his name is Terrance) our number. We establish what times were going to let him call, and we know when were going to give up the booty. Everything is planned in a way where we can't get caught up in our mess. See when were going to see Terrance, we have the plan played out with our best girlfriend ahead of time in case our man call her or try to catch us in a lie. Our man don't plan things so when he says he was with Craig and them, we catch him because Craig's dumb ass already called the house phone looking for him to go out with. Wow, you see how dumb men really are sometimes. We keep our friends up on things weeks before so there's no way she's going to call; hell, she already knows that she is the alibi. When we cheat, we normally cheat with a guy who already has a woman because we know that when we cheat with someone who already has a woman he won't get too caught up. Men are different, they cheat with a single, lonely Heffa that wants all of his time and affection and that's mistake #1.

Another thing that we do from the beginning is let Terrance know our situation from the jump without blowing up names and locations of our mate. He knows that were involved in a relationship and that were not really planning on leaving just for a little fun. When the man cheats, he never let the other woman know that he is seriously involved in a relationship and then wants to get mad when shorty start acting all territorial and possessive over his lame ass. He not telling the other woman the situation in the beginning is mistake #2.

When a real lady does her dirt, it's not with the average Joe from the same street corner our man frequents. That's word of advice for you young women out there; you never lay where you stay. Whatever you do out there in them streets, you make sure you do it discreetly because as women all we have is our name. Remember that and you will be a better person at the end of the day. I am not going to sit there and tell you not to do you because that's not reality and many of you women reading this aren't virgins, so were keeping it real. Anyway, if we hitting the streets and cheating, our side Dude lives in the Bronx while our man live in Brooklyn. Also our side Dude has something that our man lacks. Men are a little different and they don't quite understand what I call the Proximity Code or the Look Code. The Proximity Code consists of never messing with someone that lives near my proximity and the Look Code means if you're doing your dirt at least do it with a chick that I would look at and be like "damn, I would have boned her too." Men are just so thirsty for a little bit of coochie these days that they could give two shits about where the next chick lives. They'll mess with the girl that lives downstairs from you, please if he's really a dirty ass dog, he'll mess with that busted bitch that lives next door. They are just that desperate for some buns that they will not respect and adhere to the Proximity and Look Code, which is their mistake #3.

One of the many bad things about men is their mouth. Contrary to popular belief that women talk way more than men, men are the big talkers. Men talk too much when they're in a messed up situation. This is in my opinion the worse part about a cheater is when they go and sing about your ass to the side chick. They're yapping their mouths and then they wonder how they get caught when they're out there doing their dirt. The next chick doesn't have to know that you don't give good head and how you make only $30,000 per year but you're looking for a new job. They don't have to know that your shape didn't quite snap back after you had the baby but she does and you know how> because that so called man blew up all your business to the side chick not knowing that that will be her ignition when she comes straight at your ass.

I want to stress this to everyone that is reading this, running your mouth to the next person about your lover or even your ex is the worse thing that you can possibly do. If a man runs his mouth about her ass, what the hell will he do to you? It's not good to assassinate some other woman's character and I think any man that does that is a little bitch. Sorry, but I do. I remember when my first love and I broke up and he got a new chick. He told her all about my attitude bit by bit. He told her about how I was moving out of my apartment because my roommate and I had problems and then he even told her when my 18-year-old sister was pregnant. He told her my family's business and didn't even tell me. If that's not some real bitch shit then I don't know what is.

I really try not to hold things against people but that right there made me real reluctant to tell another man anything about myself. So honestly, if your man is a singer, meaning someone that likes to go run his mouth, you better watch him. Believe me, you may be the topic of his next song. When you first begin to talk to men on the phone, they're real quiet because they are listening to everything your ass is saying so they could have something to throw back in your face later on or tell the next chick. I also remember when I really liked this guy named Mel. Mel and I used to talk on the phone quite frequently, I really wanted to talk to Mel but he like most men, had a girlfriend and I really didn't want to get involved in that drama because frankly, I feel like I am too good to be the other woman.

So I continued to talk to him on the phone, we talked about everything except for his girl. Then one day, he called me up and started to run his mouth about his girlfriend. I don't know if he had an argument with her or was he just in the mood to talk but all I know by the end of the conversation I knew what projects his girlfriend lived in, where she worked at, and what college she went to (wow). Now why was that a huge mistake? Good question! Well, that was a huge mistake because for one he knew I had feelings or him. I could have been crazy and went looking for his girl and blew him up on all of our late night telephone encounters or better yet been grimey and made some stuff up on him and messed up what he had with his girl. This is to me the biggest fallacy one can make in cheating and in life in general. Luckily for him, I'm no home wrecker and I am not a hater but what if I had been?

Men think they are so smart but they are really so damn stupid. Another guy, one of my good friends by the way that I was in love with who was actually not a talker did something stupid. He told me that his cellular phone was in his girlfriend name and one day called my house phone and if you know anything about the Caller I.D. in the house; it shows the name of the person calling especially if that person's service carrier is T-mobile. The other carriers just say *Wireless Caller*. Anyway, he called and his girlfriend's name popped up on the screen and me being the curious person that I am wrote down her name so I can research her later on.

So what did I do? I placed her name in the name search on *Myspace* and just like that her page popped up. That's why it's not good to put your real name on any of those websites because you may have a stalker like me on your trail, seriously, watch your ass on *Myspace* especially not because of the killers and sexual predators but because strangers could find out so much about you and now they have your name and your face.

Anyway, I knew it was the right person because every little thing I did know about her was on her page like her school and location and she had a great poem about him on her page (how cute). I already had a name now I had a face to back it up with. Thank God I wasn't as crazy as I used to be, I just laughed at his stupidity. Boy, he better be lucky I have a heart for people because he was one person that I could have blown up because I had a lot of dirt on him. See that right there is what I call getting sloppy. He knew I liked him so why call my house phone knowing that the name may pop up or then again maybe he didn't know. So here's a tip, if you are out there creeping (and I sure hope you're not) and you know your cell phone is in your man's name you don't call your side dudes from that phone because if they have a friend that work at one of those cell phone places, he could get all the info on the contract holder like where he lives and things of that nature.

Getting sloppy is also when your man comes home with lip-gloss on his collar, open condom wrappers in his pants pocket, and text messages in his phone that's blowing up spots. Men are so stupid that they text message the next chick from their cell phones and they also are taking nasty pictures with the next chick and saving it to their phone. Now that's the funniest thing, getting caught up with one of those new technology phones like the Sidekick. And if you know anything about the Sidekick, you know that those free texts and emails can get you in even more trouble so if you plan on getting a booty call, be smart and don't do it through your phone, period.

Now that we have gone through the difference between women cheating and men cheating, let's talk a little bit about what's cheating. Remember what's cheating varies from person to person like I said earlier but let me tell you what I think is cheating. Cheating is not when your man goes to the bar after a very long and stressful day of work, gets drunk, and have sex with the woman he met at that same bar. That's considered as him slipping up because no matter how many drinks he had he should have been able to think about the relationship that he already was involved with. There were no emotional ties and he was drunk so he may not even know what he did and he most likely forgot how the girl even looked much less how she worked it. That is called unintentional sex.

He did not go to the bar looking to give up his sausage, he just got caught up in the moment and to me, that is deemed as forgivable. Hopefully, he will stop drinking because he doesn't know how to hold his liquor if he's boning chicks that he barely knows. Now there's a big problem when your man cheats and the next chick thinks she's his main chick. That right there is a hot mess and it's not forgivable. I never was a victim of my man cheating on me (meaning if he did I never knew) but I was victim of being the next chick not knowing this dude had a situation on the side and it's devastating. Whether you're the real girlfriend or the side girlfriend, it's a big mess, and you're both victims.

Ladies, please stop going after the other woman! She has been told lies just as much as you have been told lies. Sad thing about this scenario is that it will never end if you both don't leave him alone. Just like in my previous situation, we were both strong minded girls who believed that he cared about us and we kept going on but I can happily say after a long struggle, I decided to let his filthy ass go because after a while it wasn't cute anymore and like I told him while we were in bed one day, "You're boning two women and they know about each other, damn, you're pimping?" I said this because at the time, we have both found out what the hell was going on and we were still messing with him. I think it went on for a long time because it was one of those B.M.D. (yeah, Baby Mama Drama) situations and I didn't want to think that he was messing with that slouch again and she didn't want to think he was messing with my *fat* ass again either but he was.

This girl called me constantly and I let her know what was going on and she still called I guess she was thinking my story was going to change. The only difference between me and her was that I believed it after a while and I deemed it as acceptable because I remember I was still messing with my ex-boyfriend when he had a new girlfriend that he liked. See, we all know the truth but we ignore it. This girl knew how he felt about me, shit when we met up one day he dissed her ass right in front of me and she still boned him the next week telling me she was still messing with him because he apologized for embarrassing her in front of me. This girl was definitely in denial.

She really didn't understand after five years of being done wrong that this man wasn't ever planning on doing right by her. Now that's a lack of self-esteem and I hope you're reading girly, on the real, get your mind right because he's not exclusively yours and he will never be. He's everybody's and the sad thing is he does more for the side chick than he ever did for her. See men know which chick will always be there for them and that's the chick he does the worse things to. She acted like she believed everything that came out of his goddamn mouth. I later on found out that she had been in this situation plenty of times before just before when she found out he dissed the other girls not her.

The sad thing about the situation is that I never had a clue about this girl in the beginning because me and him was together a lot and we spoke on the phone almost everyday. That's the scary thing about a man. It doesn't matter if you speak or see him everyday, he could still be out there doing him. That's so crazy. These men are way too much. Anyway, thank God I never considered him to be my man but I was very opened off of him and it really taught me how grimey these dudes really could be.

Anyway, not forgivable is when your man spent $500 on a bracelet for you and he bought the next chick the same bracelet. Every time you went to work, he was smiling up in her face and the worse thing is she didn't even know anything about you. He lied to the both of you the whole entire time. Now, this is a case of a man who just don't give a damn; this is a person who you should get a first class ticket away from. He's a grimey person and he has no respect for himself and women in general. This is a dangerous man, a man that just wants his cake and wants to eat it too.

He doesn't care about your sanity, all he cares about is himself. If he's tricking on her like he's doing on you, he's really feeling this chick. Don't let him bamboozle you into thinking that she's nobody because he's a goddamned liar, he loves this girl and he doesn't care what the outcome of this situation is as long as he's with one of you guys. It's even worse when the next chick knows about you. Boy, that's real crazy. If none of these things ever happened to you, go right now and bend down and praise the Lord because you are truly blessed and if it did happened to you, figure out a way to never let it happen again. If you were the side chick and didn't know (like I once was) then you have to start researching these men and also you have to see the signs. If you never been to his house or never had his house number, chances are he has a girl. If it seems like he's only disclosing a small amount of information about himself and he's acting all secretive, go with your first gut, he probably has a girl.

Now, if you have been the one cheated on, remember that it's not your fault. It's not because you gained weight or because you work too much, it's because he's a man and cheating is in his nature. Some men cheat just for the hell of it and it doesn't matter how happy they are at home, they're like animals-they just can't control themselves. What surprised me about most of the responses I received from the survey is that most of the men admitted that they cheated just to cheat like it was some kind of hobby or something. Some also said they cheated because of the pressure they received from their so-called friends. D—Love from Brooklyn response to the question why men cheat was simply, "when you try to be faithful, you always have your boys telling you that you're too young to be with just one chick."

What was so funny about this response was that D-Love was actually 29 years-old and my question to him is if you're not ready at 29 years-old then when will you be ready also how the hell are you still being influenced by your friends when you're almost 30. I do agree that a person in their early 20's is too young to be settled down but I think it's just an excuse when a man that's almost 30 say he's just too young to be faithful. Please, I tell people like that grow up and get themselves together. Another thing I ask is why have a girlfriend in the first place if you know that you are way too young to be settled down? Why not stay single and be free to do whatever you want? I think it's because he meets a fly girl like you and he wants to put the cuffs on you while he goes out there and experiment with some other busted chick.

Some men said the obvious that men cheat because of how their women at home carry themselves. Now don't get me wrong, I believe in what Kelly from Destiny's Child said in *Cater 2 U*, "I keep my hair fixed, rocking the hottest outfits." I believe that it's very important to keep yourself together especially when you have a man because many women get comfortable and start losing it all in the name of love. You got a man all of a sudden you aint getting those toes the way you used to or you're not getting your weaves done as much because you think that you don't have anybody to impress but you do. You have to impress yourself and keeping yourself together will keep him on his toes. He will not take you for granted as much. Instead of the man telling his lady that she looks a hot ass mess and need to get it together they sit there and let you dig yourself in a big ass hole of point of now return. He won't tell you but other people around you will, and you will think they're hating but in reality they're not they just see what you don't see.

One thing that I love most about my father is that he never allows any of us, meaning my mother, my sisters, and myself, to fall off. He would be the first to let us know if were slipping before anyone else can. These men play along while their Wifey (ooh, I hate that word) stay in the house and cook and clean. They want their woman to look all plain while they go chase the female with her booty all out. Yeah ladies these men are scandalous.

Then it all comes down to sex. He makes you think he does his thang because you're not freaky enough for him. Well you suck his dick and you're open to have sex anywhere so how much more freaky does he want it? Not being freaky enough is a bullshit ass excuse that men use to make you feel like you're not on your job. You're not a prude just because you want agree with a having a threesome with him and your best friend. One of the best responses was by a Mr. Jason Sandy, he said, "Cause the only thing better than good pussy is new pussy! There is an excitement about trying something new that men can't let go, we, are too curious. Anyway, women out number men on this earth like 20 to 1. There are so many options and we guys are so indecisive because we don't wanna end up with the wrong." Mr. Sandy had one of the most honest responses and that's why his quote is in this book. I loved his answer however what I wonder about many men is why do they wife women that they know does not have something that they like physically? If you are a butt man, why marry a women does not have a big booty? They know that doing so will only set them up to cheat with a girl that does possess what they may want out of a woman.

Listen, in the end it all comes down to this, men cheat because they can. Most of the time, they don't know why they're doing it themselves. They're just doing it to have something to do or maybe it's exactly what rapper Fabolous said, "The entrée aint as good without something on the side, ya know?" The reality of it is men are animals, and until they get trained properly, they're just going to take a shit all over the place and its up to us if we want to keep their ass or get a more trained house pet. We all try to take that stray animal and change them but no matter how much we try to wash him, the piece of shit still has fleas.

If you really think about it, the question isn't really why do men cheat, the question is, why do women accept men cheating? Is it lack of self-esteem? Or is it because you grew up without a father? You see there are all kinds of reasons why women accept a cheating bastard in her world. Ask yourself, are you willing to settle and allow a man to walk all over you? It all comes down to your mind frame and what you feel intimacy and love is. Does a man really love you if he cheats on you? What I came to realize after interviewing men who was 30-years-old and under for my book is that men aren't as stupid as we think.

We must ask ourselves, are they really dumb or are they better informed than women? Are they smart to test the waters? Are they really just stray dogs or good pups waiting for the right home? It's starting to seem that both men and women want the same thing out of a relationship, however men aren't as desperate to receive it as women are. In order to figure out something as complex as cheating, you must open up your mind and look at every aspect of the subject. Doing so will then make you think, are women really the problem?

Talking to my older sister, Toni, I've come to realization that men cheat because of the way some of us women carry ourselves. There are women out there that plot on having an affair with a man just because he seems too happy with his significant other. We all know a woman that seems to only be attracted to men who already have a wife. On a side note, I strongly suggest you not to mess with a marry man but you're grown so you're going to do what you want anyway but don't say nothing when you get your ass killed because I am not married but I know a bunch of crazy ass wives who will kill a woman who tries to mess with her husband.

Anyway, it's also a fact that there's a man shortage (we outnumber men) so many women want the same man around the same time and he takes advantage of that. If all the women in the world got together and laid down the law, men would have no choice but to convert and be tamed. So remember, if you know this guy have a significant other or a wife, run because he will only bring you drama in the end and do the same damn thing to you once you get him.

Don't let these guys fool you, they know there aren't many good men left out there meaning, unattached and employed. Please, he knows that and he is just having a ball with the fact. We have to understand that straight men cheat with other women. Are we willing to settle being the other woman just to feel wanted? So now it's time for us to get together and say, "No more, enough is enough." It's time for women to stop competing with each other for a man. It's time to respect that a Queen may already be in the castle where we want to live in. It's also a time to stop blaming each other for our man's mistakes. If he's a scumbag, he is one because he wants to be. The next chick didn't put a gun to his head and say, "fuck me." He made that decision so you blame him not her.

Stop blocking your number and calling the next chick too! Remember that something in your relationship is going wrong if you have to call the next chick in the first place and if you do not listen and still call the next chick at least don't waste the phone call on insulting her. Talk to her and find out what exactly is going on and if you're the chick that's receiving the call, don't lie for these men. This distraught young lady is your way of finding out some information as well. That could be you one day, on the other line, desperate and calling the next chick. Don't lie to the female either, don't say y'all doing it if you guys are just friends. Keep it real with one another. It's time for us to unite in sisterhood and think about this, if we all came together, men will have no choice but to step it up or step it out. Remember, were all going to have our day whether it's a sunny or a rainy day. It's not really what happens that count; it's what we do after it happens. If he cheated on her with you, he will cheat on you with another chick and you can bet your rent money on that (but I don't advise you to).

When you accept a man cheating on you, you have to ask yourself, are you in love with this man or are you in love with the point of being in love? Do you just want a man to seem better than your friends or just to impress your family members? It all comes down to settling. I understand that nobody wants to be alone but that should not be the reason why you just sit there and take the bullcrap that these men are dishing out. We must be real with ourselves, were living in terrible times where it's too dangerous to be sleeping with a man that sleeps around with a bunch of chicks. That's what made me stop messing with that fool that kept going back and forth with his Baby Mama. I rather play with my vibrator or resort back to Mr. Showerhead than deal with a man that's running around on me. There are too many diseases and infections out there these days that you can get even while using a condom.

Ladies, I cant stress enough how important it is for you to protect yourself and get you and your partner tested because men that cheat carry a lot of baggage with them and you don't need to be the one suffering in the end. Just sit back and imagine all the nasty things you and him do in the bed, now think about him doing that with someone else.

Your Place in a Man's World

If your man never show up at any of your family's holiday events then chances are, he's really not your man. A real man wouldn't miss being with you on important holidays like Thanksgiving and Christmas. Family means the most to a man that time of year and if you're his girl, you're definitely his family. So ladies, just give him the old test: "Hey Honey, I want you to come to Grandma's house with me on Christmas." If he seems a little aloof or if he's silent after you ask this question then chances are he is trying to figure out a way to tell you no without hurting your feelings or he's thinking about what his real girlfriend is going to think if he misses spending Christmas with her.

If you don't spend the holiday with you man he does not give a damn about you. I know mad chicks that settle on their man not spending the holiday with them and they don't know that they might as well consider themselves as his mistress. Chances are while he's not spending his holiday with you, he's spending it with real girlfriend and you can believe that.

While were on the subject of holidays, let me express one thing that you shouldn't ever, ever, ever do and that's not bring in the New Year with your significant other. I know that you have heard this a million times and think it's just a myth but believe me it's true. The first year that I did not bring in the New Year with my ex-boyfriend that was the year that we called it quits after being in a relationship for six years. New Years is the beginning of a new life, hell, a new you and not spending it with the person you love is a great indication of you living your life without that person.

I know you maybe thinking that it's just a coincident that we broke up on that same year but I deny that. On that New Years, I counted down the numbers with my father's side of the family, I counted and counted and for some reason what seemed to be a great night, began to go all wrong. The whole night people kept asking me where he was because they were so used to us being together every minute of the day and I had to explain that he was working. I mean, I had proof he really was at work but it still dampened my world that he was not there spending the New Year with me.

I remember asking him why did he have to work and he said because everybody took off and since he was the only one without a *family* (meaning a wife and kids) he had to take the fall. I understand that when you're young, jobs think that you should be the one to work on important holidays but why didn't he take off a long time ago before New Years? Why didn't he explain that he actually did have a family that he wanted to spend his holiday with? I guess he didn't think about it or better yet, he probably didn't want to spend his New Years with me or maybe he needed that double holiday pay, I don't know. Well, maybe that's the problem when you're dating a Security Guard.

This brings me to a very important part of this book which is supposed to tell you the truth and open up your eyes to bullcrap and uplift you from the pain, the lies, the confusion, and overall the game. *You can't force yourself to be an important asset in someone else's life.* All my life I strived to make myself feel important in everything I did from school, work, friendships, relationships, etc. but after being single and dating for a year or so I realized you cant make yourself important in a man's life, he has to feel you already are and make it his business to show that to you.

For most of my relationship with my ex boyfriend, I was very important in his life. I knew it and never had to question my existence in his world but things changed when I started to deal with this guy named Jason. This is the person I dedicate this book to most (now that I think about it) because he showed me how messed up a dude could treat you even when you tried your best to keep them and make them happy. He did some of the same stuff that I talk to you about in this book except he did it on the down low.

He also taught me how a man could have a big, juicy sirloin steak on his plate in front of him but still beast for the left over franks on the stove. That right there taught me how to love myself even more and realize that when these men do dirt on you or treat you like the average chick that its just apart of them feeling inferior of you and just taking advantage of the way you feel about them. He did lots of things to me but guess what, I taught myself how to be strong and now I could say that I am a better woman today because of the losers I have encountered in my life.

I once almost sold my soul while trying to make a man feel like he needed me. I really believed that I was somebody that was necessary in Jason's life. I always knew in the back of my mind when I met his family that he wasn't ready for me to meet them. He really wasn't ready because he really didn't believe that we were actually that serious enough to take that step but I forced it. I always knew that he didn't want to attend every one of my family's events with me but he did in fear of losing me. I knew he didn't want to diss his Baby's mother for me that time we confronted him but he did.

None of that means shit now because in reality, I wasn't as important as I thought I was or basically felt I should have been. I know now that I wasn't that important because I had to always remind him of my importance. See, if you're important to someone, you don't have to reassure him or yourself that you are it would just be evident by the way he looks at you and the way he acts towards you. He took my attitude of importance as arrogance but I was truly trying to hold my own territory down and keep the man I felt I loved.

Unfortunately, no matter what I tried to do or say, Jason never felt worthy of me. He always felt that I was too good for him. He displayed this in his actions and by the things he said. I remember in one of our earlier on conversations he ended it with saying, "Just never treat me like I'm not good enough for you." I always questioned why he would even think I would ever feel that way. Even though he hasn't accomplished as many things that I had at the time, I was still crazy about this guy. This man made me believe in men and love again. I was totally smitten by him. He exuded sexiness in the way he walked and the way he talked. He seemed very confident. He was very masculine and his body was serious. Hell, this man held me like I was the softest thing on earth. I mean he looked up to me and gave his all when we made love (yeah, I was open).

All this is good but Jason was young (2 years younger than I was) and not really ready to settle down and do whatever it took to hold down a grown ass woman like myself. He was used to those dumb ass, insecure, don't-give-me-nothing-just-give-me you broads and didn't know how to hold it down. He, like most men, just wanted everything to come so easy to him however that was not my style at all. I tried to explain to him that he had to work to get me and work even harder to keep me. So ladies, remember if you're not his everything, you might as well be nothing to him because sadly your position on the totem pole would never change unless he decides to change it and who knows how long that may take. I mean really, how many times do you have to touch the stove to know that it is hot?

Overall ladies, whether its spending holidays with you or treating you like the queen you deserve to be, a man is not worthy of you if he doesn't make you his all and show you that you are the most important person in his life. It is a man's responsibility to treat you very well and to do everything he needs to do to make you happy. If you are sitting there after years of being in a relationship and still wondering your place in his life then you might as well consider the relationship as done. Always remember, if you're not first in your man's world, you're last and that's a spot you should never aspire to be at.

Men Not Buying the Cow

There comes a time in every relationship where your mate is coming over to your house every night or vice versa. Then one of you comes up with the great idea of getting an apartment together. You think, Why not? Your rent will be cheaper, you will get to see each other more often, you will get to see the way your man lives before you even could think about marrying him; you know the old saying: *You don't know a person until you live with them.* Look at people who have been friends for years and all of a sudden they move in with each other and have a big fall out; so you know that quote is true. So you decide that it will be for the best for the two of you to move in together.

Moving in with your man will always start off great.

You two sit there and look through the newspaper for apartments. You two even meet after work to take a look at a few places. He wants a big living room for game night with the boys and you want enough closets to fit your oh—so-many pairs of shoes. You guys look and look and look until finally you both settle on a place; a 1½ bedroom apartment which is in good proximity to both of you guy's jobs. Your good-with-his-hands man promises he would build you a closet from the half bedroom so that you would be happy. You think you made the right decision because you were paying way more money for a place of your own and he was there every night anyway.

He feels relieved because he has access to the coochie anytime now and he doesn't have to troop it all the way to your apartment in the middle of the night to have it. It all starts out as being cute, you cook and he washes the dishes. You handle the laundry and he take cares most of the bills. You're happy and hoping that this method of doing things will continue once you two get married.

This goes on for months; you two wake up in the morning, eat cereal together, and then ride the train together to work. You rush home after work to make sure his food is cooked and he comes home to eat it. Y'all talk about work, watch a little television, get in a little sex before bed, and then you two go off to sleep. Everything seems to be going great then all of a sudden something happens. That little thing that you've both promised will never happen that something is called *comfort*. Four years has past and the newness of living together has worn off and now you guys are accustomed to each other. How did you get so comfortable? You're no longer wearing them sexy thongs to bed; you're wearing some big ass sweatpants and a very long shirt. You're too tired from work to get all dolled up and besides whom do you have to impress? You forgot how you used to wake up ten minutes before to take the rollers out of your hair or the way you used to wake up and brush your teeth before you talked to him in the morning, he'd better like it.

How did he get comfortable? He starts out by leaving his clothes and those stinky socks from the night before on the floor thinking that you (the maid) is going to come behind him and pick it up, hey you don't have anything else better to do. He no longer take care of the dishes when you cook, he considers that to be women work. He's no longer talking about that house you two were supposed to buy years ago, he's comfortable with where he's at and besides it's cheaper to rent. Now you went from honey-mooning to getting comfortable within only a few years but the real problem of shacking up is *there are no longer any talks of marriage*. You two talked about marriage when you first hooked up and you specifically remember him saying that you two were going to get hitched once y'all lived together for a bit and saved enough money to do so. Now you two have been playing house for 5 years and it seems as if this relationship is going on slow motion.

What you didn't realize is men do not understand the difference between *play* and *real* life. Now after talking to your close friends and family members, you are furious about the way you see the relationship heading. You approach him and ask him, "Where do you see this relationship going?" He explains to you that you two have a lot of time to get married and that he already sees you as his wife so what's the rush? What he's not going to tell you is that 99% of the time, he has no intentions on marrying you. You two have been together so long that there's no point of getting married. Marriage is to him is now just a piece of paper. He is wondering what would change if he did decide to marry you and think about it, y'all already share a bed, already have a joint bank account, and you already love each other so what's the big issue?

The issue is he's getting those buns every night without having any papers on the coochie. He could die in a car accident the day or tomorrow and it doesn't matter how many years you have been with this man, you could be left with nothing but sweet old memories. You're not his wife so you do not have a say on any of the funeral arrangements, his immediate family does. It will be like your relationship with this man never existed. He shouldn't only marry you because of the security that you would have if something happens to him, he should marry you because you are worth being his bride and not just his plaything or his girlfriend. If you're good enough to lamp around the house with then you're good enough to marry.

Then there's the issue of the amount of years you have invested your heart, soul, and mind into this one person. Think about your relationship as if it was a job job. Pretend you were on a job for ten years and within those ten years, you never received a promotion or a generous raise, wouldn't you feel like a fool for staying at that job for so long? Why should you work to keep something that is not going anywhere? I have heard of too many stories of men being with women umpteen years and never marrying them and when they break up with their long-term lover, they go and marry the next chick who they have only dated a year.

See the next chick aint going to take that bullcrap from him. She wants to know what the stars are saying about her future. You, on the other hand, wanted to be nice but like I say all the time about niceness, it's a bad quality to have at times, and that's why people get dissed and dismissed. I know a couple that have been together since the 70's. Three children and 30 years later he moves out of state and marry another woman who he met at his job. This all happened in a matter of two years. Something like this happening to you will crush your soul and make you want to kill somebody. I know I would have been that chick you always imagine at every wedding, coming through interrupting things.

Someone would have been ready to shoot my ass before the night was over. But hey, if you're one of those women who aren't beasting to get married or like things the way they are in your long-term relationship then keep doing things your way (it aint broke so why fix it) but if you're one of those women who dreamed of that big fairy tale wedding with all your best friends and sisters as bridesmaids then put your foot down and make sure he buys the cow if he's ready to drink the milk. Better yet start out by doing the right thing and don't live with your man in the first place. I know you love him and I know rent is very expensive these days but you have to be smart and not play the wife role. Matter of fact here's a better suggestion, get a roommate!

Never Ever Accept Being Disrespected

The last thing you need when you're trying to get your mind right is a man that disrespects you. This is one *sermon* I preach to all of my friends because this is the most devastating fallacy one could make against you.

As we all already know respect is more important than love and twice as important as sex in a relationship. Once a man loses that respect for you, you might as well consider the relationship as over. We could discuss disrespect until the cows come home but do you really know what disrespect is? Once a man gets mad and calls you a bitch the respect is now gone. A bitch turns into a fat bitch, a wack bitch, a stupid bitch, etc. Take it from somebody that father called them a bitch since they were about 9 years old, the verbal rants will never stop. All men knows that calling a woman a bitch is the most disrespectful thing that they could do. Their mother teaches them this at a very young age.

These men sit and want to smile all in your face but as soon as they feel threatened by you as a woman. They feel the need to call you the worse name in the book after the C word (ask your grandmother if you don't know what that word is).

When a man calls you a bitch, he is being very demeaning to you and basically shitting on your good name. And don't let them really call you a bitch with the lips clasped, it comes out even worse. It is not that vital when a man calls me a bitch because I have heard it all my life. "Wash the dishes, bitch!" or "Bitch I put you in this world." I am not assassinating my father's character or anything but by him calling my sisters and I bitches our whole life, it has not only messed up our mentality as ladies but it has prepared us for the disrespect that may come in the future. The sad thing is hearing this word being said so much in your childhood makes you think that this type of behavior is acceptable and it's not.

As women, we are the nurturers and the rulers of the earth and no woman deserves to be called out of her name. So what at times were a little fussy and our attitudes are a little messed up, hell we have gained the right from getting periods to the extra hormones that our body naturally absorbs, we have gained our right to not always being in the mood for someone else's mess. You have some men that come out of their face for reason just because they do not get what they want from you or because you didn't answer your phone quickly enough.

Ladies, please remember that you're not a female dog, a gardening tool, or any other defamed, disrespectful name a man decides to place on you. You are a woman, you're strong, independent, and you could be alone if you had to. The first time a man commits this sin let him know right away without blinking, calmly that he better not ever come out of his face again and that that type of behavior is unacceptable. Let him know that you're not playing because if you laugh about this he is going to think its okay and if you're screaming too much over it; it will only create an even bigger issue. I don't know if it's because of the verbal rants that my father proposed on me but I cant even except when a man's tone in his voice gets a little high. If you around me with any man except for maybe my father, you get over hear me saying, "watch your tone" or "disrespect me," and believe me I am so serious.

Now let's be serious, sometimes when a man calls you out of your name it's a form of foreplay. I understand that believe me I do.

When a man says, "Give me that pussy, bitch," that may be the words that may turn you on sexually but make sure that he understands that he should keep that kind of animalistic talk in the bedroom, I understand that he listens to a Cam'ron CD every now and then but keep the vulgarity out of your everyday life. He better just lip-sync those words by himself in the bathroom.

A woman being disrespected by a man is one of my pet peeves. I hate it but sadly many of you women think it's so cute and its not. It starts out with name calling, then it goes to pushing, then it goes to hitting and before you know it you will be in a 5 year abusive relationship with nowhere to turn. Ladies, you must understand that little things in life become bigger over time. We all have control over a situation at first but before you know it you're so left behind with nowhere to go and no way out. This is a line that I have been saying since I was kid, what you except in the beginning will be your down fall in the end—this quote especially valuable for my young ladies that is reading this book. I am going to keep it totally real with you, never, ever, except any build of that a man may throw at you. You will live to regret it, if the first time he disrespects you whether it is breaking the code by having one of his other chicks call you or whether its him getting mad calling you a slut bag whore, give him his verbal warning because if he's a disrespectful bastard, there is going to be a second time, you leave his ass alone because believe me its going to only get worse.

Young women, you have to understand that once you accept bullcrap from a man and act as if nothing happened and everything is okay, he will look at you like you're a punk and feel like he could do anything to you and your ass is still there not going anywhere. You don't want to be looked up to as the slouch in his life. If you began practicing this behavior now at a young age, you would avoid the bullcrap that may come down the road later, trust. You're young, you're beautiful, and you could do things better than I did, your older sister, or your mother did. When you see a woman so desperate that she's taking every piece of crap a man is throwing at her, look at that. Observe that, and just learn from their mistakes, I know I have.

You may slip up a time or two but now this part of the book to your head because believe me you're going to see me in your local mall or movie theatre and say thank you. I know that's what I do to the woman who have motivated me and showed me that you never let your esteem get so low that you let a man spit on you and make you even sicker in the game. Now for my mature women who know all this information but need a little touch up, what you accepted in the past doesn't have to be what takes over your life in the present. All the times you let a man disrespect you and you stayed, forget about it! Like a New Year's resolution, start your life over and promise yourself from this day forward you'll never accept a man cursing you out just for kicks, slapping the hell out of you, or dealing with other women on the side. Frankly my dear, you're too old for the nonsense and you already tried and tried to work with him, so you already know. Honey, he aint never going to change, its only going to get worse. He will do even more disrespectful things to you because after a while he's going to think that you like the abuse; especially since you're not doing anything drastic to change his behavior.

My friend Sheila and I were on the phone one day and we were talking about how I have a low-tolerance for bullshit (bullshit makes me itch) and how many women are different. Everyone has their own breaking point where they say enough is enough and I agree with this. I have had my share of bullcrap but I didn't just sit and accepted it. I worked on getting rid of it don't matter how hard it is. So during our conversation, a good question came up, why do some people accept disrespect while others don't? It's real simple. Many women that accepts verbal and physical abuse have saw women in their life get pimp smacked a couple of times and accepted or they had mothers that let their fathers or the men in their life do whatever and get away with it. I can't speak for everyone's household but I can definitely speak for my own. In my own household, my father was the king over king. Anything that he said went in my household and my mother never questioned anything he said, I mean my father could tell my mother to cook a full course meal at 3:00 am and she would do it. I always thought it was my household but it isn't, it goes down in many households and why? Because this is what was taught, the man is the ruler, the man is the king but we never sat and ask ourselves, who made these rules? Now in many two-parent households the woman of the household does whatever it is that the male says do.

Many of our parents were raised old school where the man was in charge and women were to be seen and not heard just as if they were children. It's good to have old values and morals but it's bad too in a sense. If you really think about it, it's not right when a man could do and say anything and the woman just sits there and allows any kind of abuse, disrespect to happen in the relationship towards the children. I'm not saying any names but I know a household with a similar situation.

In this household there is a mother and father (let's say their names are Cindy and David). Now Cindy is more of a quiet woman who enjoys a strong man to rule her world. She is considered a passive aggressive sort of person but she does have a temper it just takes ten years to get it out of her. Then you have David. David has what we call a military-mentality where as he was raised to believe that women must never talk back to the man. He believes that women are supposed to cook, clean, and take care of the children. The only thing hat he does think the women can do is work if she pleases because two checks are better than one. Now you know opposites attract so Cindy and David get marry and have three children, all girls. Wow! So now you know David is a very aggressive man and having three children especially girls has made his attitude never worse because now he has to deal with four different females in one household, four different attitudes, and whatever else that comes with raising three daughters in the ghetto. Now what happens next? David has no clue on raising daughters, he has a family full of men and he promises himself that his children will not grow up depending on a man and being weak, so he flips the treat-your-daughter-like-a-princess attitude and begin to raise his daughters with a pit-bull mentality.

So he decides to curse his daughters out whenever he gets mad. He decides to slap the hell out of them as well and he begins to embarrass them in front of their friends whenever he gets a chance. He flips out like this all the while spoiling them and introducing them to the upper middle class life thinking that he's doing the right thing for his family. Not throwing that he is acting sort like a pimp when he smack up his shoes and label the women in his life as bitches, sluts, etc. This man is thinking that he is making his children strong because it's a hard knock life for girls growing up in the 21st century. He is applauding himself for being like his friends and walking out on his responsibility. He thinks he's doing such a great job especially because his first daughter graduated from college and is now a big shot at a financial firm and married with no children. The woman of this relationship doesn't like the way he carries on in the household. She doesn't like when he curses the girls out and calls them all types of names. He used to smack her and curse her out too but she found a way to get him to stop because this bitter man knows that he doesn't have anyone else that will love him and take his crap like she will. She's happy because she has everything that she has ever dreamt about as a child: a husband, a house, and her girls. She feels like she has done her job as a mother and a wife; she has set a good example and also agrees that tough love makes you stronger because that was the same way she was raised only her father didn't slap her and call her a fat bitch, so she really doesn't see his behavior as such a big deal. She doesn't have any intentions on trying to change him because she doesn't want to take his manhood away and she knows that he is doing it from his heart because they have had countless heart to hearts regarding this situation.

So, what's the main problem in this situation? No one has discussed how this situation may have affected the children. What do the children think? How do they feel? How does this type of "abuse" affect their interactions with men? Well first of all when you have three different children, one situation can affect them all differently. All three children agree that their father has been out of control since the eighties when he thought it was discipline to whip their ass with extension cords and call them bitches in front of other people including their boyfriends. They that it's impossible to talk to their mother about the situation because she's already so brain washed from this man that it is sickening. They were so embarrassed growing up in this situation that they had warned their friends about his behavior before they visited so they won't be shocked when he went off on one of his verbal tirades. The girls consider their mother as a weak woman because she lets anything goes down without saying a word.

Witnessing her passive behavior has placed a strain in their mother-daughter relationship and furthermore loses respect for her and not takes her advice when it comes down to men. They feel like she never protected them like she could of. They understand that he thinks that he is making them strong by acting this way but they still believe he needs counseling. The mother also doesn't realize that she is fueling the father's power by telling her daughter's personal business to him.

Now when it comes down to the affects of growing up around this rowdy behavior, it affects all three of the girls differently. One grew up and emulated her mother by allowing a man to rule her world. She turns out to be the one that likes it when a man takes over and she ends up being attracted to men who disrespect her. She goes through plenty of trial and tribulations and doesn't really know where to turn. She's sensitive yet she's strong at heart. She is motivated and ends up successful but she's weak at the same time. She gets married to the first guy who doesn't disrespect her. The second daughter will rebel against her father. She's the daughter that joins a gang, get pregnant at an early age, and cause the most aggravation to the family. She to, like her sister and mother, is a sucker for love however she allows a man to be in charge only up to a point. Like her father, she has a hitting problem often times hitting her male counterpart first which creates a domestic problem for herself. She is in the middle of being weak and strong but other people view her as more strong than weak. Everyone considers her to be a pit-bull but people that really know her could identity her weakness in a heartbeat. This daughter searches for love in everything she does because of the lack of love and attention at home.

So you have the daughter that acts like the mother, then the daughter that's in the middle, so what's next? The daughter whose attitude is mostly branded by the crazy ass household; the bitch of the family. The one that finds everything wrong in everything and everybody. This daughter aims to be different from not only her mother but her sisters too. She believes that every woman around her is weak and she does everything in her power so that she doesn't end up like them. She dismisses men as soon as they even think about disrespecting her. Like her father, she is a verbally abusive person in the relationship. She has an ideology about love that makes her look unrealistic to those around her. She's very aggressive and she goes after anything that she wants. She is usually the one that approaches a man for their number. She has a control problem, she wants to rules everything around her and if she doesn't, she isn't interested.

Although she is very stronger than most women, she wears her heart on her sleeve as well but unlike her siblings, she loves only a small amount of people. She's the sister that had about one or two boyfriends because she doesn't have trust in men. She doesn't see how disrespectful she is to a man and how she lives her life only to break down a man and make him feel like a bitch. This is the person that still holds resentment against both of her parents and agrees that the way she was raised has helped her become the strong woman that she is today. She also feels that she will never be happy and never have a complete family life. So which kid wins? The one who's in the middle of personalities? The strong one? The answer is nobody wins. I hope this will help you remember why it isn't good for a child to witness a weak mother and a father who is not checked on the way he raises his kids. As women we praise men that raise their children but what we don't realize is that that's their responsibility, women have been doing it for years, raising kids and leaving their mark. Women, its time for us to stop accepting disrespect and remember that there is a little girl out there watching you (even if you have daughter or not). So remember Homegirl, you're a role model. Girl, Get, your mind right!

Realizing that Sex is just Mental

We all want to be big whores like men but no matter what we say or do, there will always be a double standard. No matter what we think, we can't go have sex with 5 men at the same time without being branded as a slut-bag. We have to understand some major things about sex. The first major one is just because you have sex with you doesn't mean that he cares about you and your well being. We must stop mistaking a good piece of bun-bun with love. I know that when he's on top of you, that dick feels so good but don't be fooled. A man that doesn't love you cannot possibly make love to you. He can slow stroke you but he can't make love to you. We must stop thinking a man cares for us just because he screws us. It's time for women to understand that sex is all mental.

The sad thing about being a woman is that we can't hump without emotions like men can, we have too much to lose. The best thing to do when you're open off of someone sexually but can't figure out how you feel about them mentally is to step back from the bedroom and ask yourself what it is about this man that you truly adore. If you're stuck with this question then you already know the answer.

Ladies, don't get gassed up because he's hitting it from the back all nice and tender while holding on to your breast and nibbling on your ear because studies show that most men favorite sexual position is doggy style. Doggy style is not only their favorite position because the man is in total control but because it is a very emotion-less position where the man is penetrating the vagina while looking at your backside. He can see the waves in the booty but there is no eye contact amongst you two and it's easier for him to focus while he stroking and stomach you. He doesn't have to look at your face so it makes it easier for him to imagine having sex with another woman of his dreams like Beyonce' or Halle Berry. The doggy style position is also many men favorite position because that position makes them cum faster. 50 Cents was definitely right, these men are into sex and not into making love. These men now a days are not focused on making you satisfied, they're just worried about them-selves so be careful and don't get all emotional and caught up in the moment of lust.

Lastly, we must watch whom we allow in our bedrooms because when we have sex with someone where actually feeling the inside of their souls. The spirits aren't really transferred when you have pro-tected sex; it's more when you bone raw. I know you have heard the saying that the body is the temple (and it's true). We must be care-ful about who we allow in our bedrooms because many of our part-ners carry spirits that we may not want to possess.

Have you ever started acting like a man (personality wise) that you were having sexual intercourse with? Or better yet, have you ever had sex with a depressed person and all of a sudden you started to feel a little depressed? That's an example of transferring of spirits. Remember ladies, when a man and a woman make love; the man is implanting his spirit (the penis) into the female's world (the vagina). So ladies, remember we must watch whom we sleep with and see past the penis.

Leave the Hustlers and Jailbaits Alone!

I know you ladies out there love your Thug Fizzles. Yes, Thug Fizzles aka Thugs, Gangsters, Gs, Bad Boys, etc. but if you ever want to get your mind right, you have to get serious and get rid of the bullcrap in your life. Like it or not but Thugs will bring you down one way or another. Think about it, when you date men who are Hustlers aka drug dealers; they begin to put on this 50 Cent/Jay-Z persona. They act like they're some celebrity or something living the fast life with money, cash, and hoes. They always like girls like you, yeah, that ride or die chick but face it, if you have one of these dudes that's caught up in this lifestyle, you will always go through drama.

You know as soon as a hood Negro gets a little cash, girls want to be all up in their face; so even if your man wants to be true to you, temptation will come along and he will cheat on you. He's barely home so he will not have time to spend with you. This Hustler will spend all of his cash on the latest Jordan's and the hottest chains that he sees the other hood dudes with. He used to be a great guy, very motivated. He loved life and always loved money, however he felt like the $7.00 an hour job wasn't his style. He wants big, fast, and tax-free dollars so he can live the life he has always dreamed of. He wants to do right but he says the game keeps calling his name. He saw how the characters in *Menace to Society* and *New Jack City* turned out but it didn't scare him from joining the drug game, it only turned him on to it.

With no health coverage, no pension, no savings for the future, and no real established credit, he thinks he is fly. He thinks that those $195 jeans and $500 coat will take him to high places. So what he doesn't have his own place, he drives a Mercedes Benz that looks mean in the summertime. He doesn't care about the fact that he doesn't have any education, he's too cool for school; his degree from the school of hard knocks will get him by. He doesn't care about where he will be in the future; he's just living for today. Then there's you, the Hustler's wife better known in the hood as Wifey.

You loved him before he got on to the street life and you believe that he's doing this for you guy's future. You are the woman he talks about his future with and you know there are no retired drug dealers, yet you sit still and say nothing. You know what he does is wrong but still no matter what your family or friends says, you're turned on by the fact that he is a so-called street Dude. You enjoy the benefits of his hard work; you enjoy the shoes and the sneakers he buys you every week and love to feel his chain smack on your ass when he's hitting it from the back. So what, you know he aint really thugged out, hell he ran when his own brother was getting jumped last summer in the park, but you love him anyway. You love how he always talking about busting his guns; you love that you know all about the crack game and how much money you don't make by being the corner boy. Hell, this dude got your ass so sprung that you snuck a few balloons in your big Louis Vuitton bag to transport for him.

You did it because you liked feeling needed and seeing the look on his face when you told him you did what he has asked of you and you did it without making one single mistake. You like bragging to your friends about how he gave you $400 for your new Michael Kors Coat even though he just spent $500 just last week on your new Gucci pumps. You like all the things he buys you, however, you're getting older and now realize that you are tired of living in the projects and you want a way out. You want to stack your ends so that you can buy a house. So now you are starting to wonder, what is your future with this drug dealer? Is he ever going to outgrow this? How could you both grow together?

The answer is simple, there is no future with this man unless he straightens up his act and realizes that if he doesn't work, he doesn't eat. He has to be just like all the rest of us, get off his ass and make that almighty dollar. If he spent as much time becoming a real entrepreneur instead of a hood booger, he will be okay but he isn't. He is satisfied as long as he looks fresh and gets the props he wants from the people around him. The more he looks at the videos on *BET,* the more he gets into this lifestyle; hey he wants to be balling too. He sees the cars, the women, the money, the jewels, and realizes that a regular job just aint going to cut it. His excuse for not getting a job is that he hasn't found one yet that pays enough money. Well newsflash, with no education or work history, how much money does he plan to make?

Your hood-hop man hasn't had a job since High School so he has no current pay stubs or income that he has paid taxes on; so basically he is completely shot of helping you acquire a mortgage. Let me explain something to you, there isn't a bank in America that is going to let him get a loan for a house in his name. No money saved, no credit and no work history, equals living in his Mama's house forever. It's hard to get an apartment with no credentials these days much less a house, are you kidding me?

Then you both lose something that has always been a great factor in your relationship: common interest. While he's chasing street dreams, you are motivated to climb the corporate ladder. All of a sudden him keeping his Timberlands on while y'all make love is no longer appealing. The fact that he does not have anything in his closet to wear to a funeral is starting to disgust you. It is sickening to you that he will pay over $200 for a pair of sneakers but refuses to pay for a button up to go to an interview is making you sick. A few years ago, you thought this was all a phase but now he's hitting 27-years-old and not a damn thing has changed from five years ago. He swears to you that he loves you but the Tiffanys and Nancys of the hood keeps calling and telling you that their screwing him and he's tricking that dough on them as well. You ask yourself why do you keep taking his mess but you do nothing about his indiscretions because, hey, you love him. What you don't know is that the only thing worse than you is a chick waiting for her man while he is locked up in jail. You need to realize that a man that's caught up in this life is not in touch with reality. He is not familiar with hard work, he just wants everything easy and for that reason alone, you have to let him go.

One day this guy I know asked me a very good question. He asked me if I was his girl and he got locked up and had to do a bid for 5 years, would I wait for him. I thought to myself and said real quickly, "No." I know I seem a little harsh and it seems like I'm not a rider for my man but I'm just keeping it real. I'm not going to even bamboozle him or myself into believing that bullcrap; I mean I'm thinking like a man. Ask yourself this, ladies, would a man wait five years for you? Hell, he wouldn't even wait five months, much less five whole goddamn years. So why should I?

I mean I am not going to let a man I love just rot in jail without giving him a little psychological and financial support but I am not going to sit there and let love pass me by because he's caged in like some animal. Please if he cared about me he would have never broken the law and placed himself into that situation in the first place. I think it's very selfish for a man to even expect his woman to wait for him to get out. I don't know what's happening in the next five minutes much less five years. If he love you, he would let you do you because he knows that he is locked up and can not help you sexually or financially.

He wants you to wait five years while he's in jail only for him to come out and shit on you for the next chick; I don't think so. I'm not going to go hard visiting and writing a dude and he gets out and forget all about you, sorry. Half of the times they have another chick up there visiting them anyway so save your time and money and don't do it to yourself. Why do you have to stop your life just because he messed up? Life is too short for these kinds of hang-ups. You deserve to be happy and not allowing someone else to come into your life because he is locked up doesn't make any kind of sense.

That's like if you were eight months pregnant when he got convicted and when he comes out your child is now five years old; your child wouldn't know him and after he's been locked up for five years, you don't either. Oh no, you cant go that route and think about it after being incarcerated for that many years, what job is he going to get? Please think about that, ladies! Some men clean up their act when they're released but others just fall their ass right back into the trap the system designed.

Waiting for that man to come out of prison will only hinder your growth. While waiting, you're only thinking about the past and the good times. Now, I am not trying to down any women that is out there who is waiting for their man to be released from prison. This is not about getting upset, this is about motivating you and in order to motivate you, we have to keep it real. If you are out there waiting for your man and doing it faithfully (that means without a little friend or Mr. Dicky on the side), I commend you because you're definitely a better woman than I am but if you are not waiting, don't be ashamed! I am with you. There are reasons why some women stay and wait. The main reasons are the babies: we all love the kids. You want them to know who their fathers are and don't want to bring other men around them. Great! That is so cute but think like this, you could still move on and make sure your children knows who their father is and you don't have to bring every man that you bang around your children. Go on a date, have fun, but make sure you take your children on visits to see their father and keep some pictures of him around the house too.

Some women wait because they're married and believe in their vows; to love for better or for worse. Now that's really nice, I could respect that. That's the only situation that I could see you sticking around for and besides you can get conjugal visits so it won't be that bad. To my brothers that are locked up in jail, I want y'all to know that I love y'all dearly and I hope you can return to the outside life and do your thing, I really do, but I have some questions and concerns about you brothers.

One of my many concerns regarding these incarcerated men is the psychological affect that prison may have on their mentality but most of all it's the homosexual activity that happens inside of the jail. You can say whatever you want but if a man is used to getting coochie on the regular then get locked up for ten years, they got to be hitting something within those years. Whether it's a Correction Officer or a fellow inmate, they're doing something to relieve that sexual tension. Please don't say jerking off because I mean I am a strong believe of masturbation (why let someone do what you could do yourself) but it gets really boring after a while; you need that good stuff, that real gushy stuff. I may be closed minded or just pure horny but I couldn't wait, at this point of my life, ten years to have sex. I got to hit something up so imagine how a man feels. Most down low brothers derive from the penitentiary. They don't think their homosexual because they are the one slamming that tool in the hole but they are. Now that brings us into a whole new situation, men having sexual relations with other men in jail and that makes me think about one thing, *Aids*.

According to an article in the New York Times, *Testing Increases in City Jails and Hospitals*, testing increased in New York City because the number of positive tests more than doubled to 11,520 from 720. So yes, there are people in jail that has Aids and if your man is unaware of this and have sexual relations with a fellow inmate, he is placing himself and you in danger of acquiring *HIV*. So like I tell most people and myself don't make yourself a victim! There are too many single (ok, well there's some single men) in the outside world waiting for a good woman like yourself. Don't stress yourself over a man that may end right back in jail. Forget about the bad boys if they refuse to reform, they will only be your downfall. You're trying to get your mind right, you don't need their problems you have your own. In other words, give a good man a chance. I know they may seem corny at first but hey; at least, you can have a future with one of them and grow to your best potential. Leave the slackers alone and upgrade yourself!

Doing Things Differently

Sometimes you have to do things differently to get things you never had.

That's something that Dora's (my friend) brother told us one day during one of his *lectures* that he gave Dora. He wasn't even talking to me but when he said it but I took it very personal. During this time I was very depressed about the way things were going on in my life and I needed to find another way and nothing that I was doing at the time was working for me. I began by looking inside of myself to find out what exactly was it that was bothering me.

At this time I began to realize that you have to worry about yourself because in the end, all you have is yourself and Jesus. So I broke down my life in 3 pieces: Physical, Emotional, and Financial. I looked at my strength and weaknesses in each category. In the physical department, I was proportioned rather well (big breast and a big booty to go along with it); in the emotional department, I didn't welcome many dudes in my world therefore I didn't have many spirits lurking in my mind and in the financial department, I was gainfully employed for over a year (something that I have never achieved before) and finally established a stable living. That was all good but then it was time for the real nitty-gritty.

I began to look really deep into the negative things in my life and I realized that I had plenty of things that needed to be changed. In the physical department I was overweight; I was only 5'2 and weighed over 175 pounds. In the emotional department, I realized that although I didn't love many men, I loved too hard and believed that once a man was in a relationship with me, it was forever until I decided it was over. In the financial department, I made a decent salary but never saved a dime and my credit wasn't even sufficient enough to get an apartment in my name without a co-signer.

You see I could talk about the cons of my life because honestly, I worked and still is working on trying to be a better me. So what did I do? I got my ass on a better eating schedule (I stopped eating after a certain time), I ate less fast food and I enrolled my ass in fitness boot camp where I didn't lose much weight (because I cheated and skipped some days of a workout) but I did lose body fat and my body did looked more defined. I began to write at this time and started realizing that nothing lasted forever and there wasn't one human being on earth that I owned. You know what, when it all comes down to it, some things are just not meant to be. I began to think, think, and think until I couldn't think anymore.

Lastly, I decided to start taking care of my priorities and started paying bills off of my credit report. If you need your credit report, get a free one at www.freecreditreport.com or buy yours from www.experian.com. It is very important to pay your bills; it's not cute when you rock a $600 bag and you owe money to every creditor and don't have even $60 in the bank. Paying off your bills right away will not get rid of your debt right away but it will show other prospect creditors that you're starting to become responsible. I also opened two revolving accounts (department credit cards) at *Target* and *J.C. Penny.* I used them and paid them right away so that other companies could see I had good standing accounts.

So ladies, pay your bills. I would like to stress this especially my young ladies while you still have a chance to be financially stabled, how important credit is. Credit is what controls the world. I used to not give a damn about how many phone bills I ran up in my name and didn't pay but it all caught up to me one day just like my parents told me. I remember I wanted this badass apartment in the

Bronx where my friend lived at the time. The apartment had parquet floors and two huge closets in the bedroom. It was like a young woman's dream and I wanted it. All I needed to get the apartment was a credit score of 600 (mine was 520). So basically, I didn't get the apartment. That basically hurt my soul and I felt like an ultimate loser but I convinced myself that it probably wasn't meant to be. Credit is important and without it you wouldn't be able to get a great mortgage rate or buy a brand new car so ladies let's get it together.

Doing things differently is basically doing stuff that you normally wouldn't do. I would have normally not cared about anything that I thought I couldn't change but now I do. I am still struggling off and on with my weight but I have maintained paying my bills on time. When it comes down to my emotions, believe me it's off and on. It's like I care but I really don't care as much as I used to about people. I mean, life is one big emotional rollercoaster, you feel differently about people at different times. No matter how hard you try, some men whether you boned them or not would always have a place in your heart. It's just now you have to think with your mind and not your heart.

So whatever it is in your life that you feel like you struggle with, believe in yourself and change it. Do the extraordinary—do what is not expected of you! If that man expects you to call after he hung up on you, teach his ass a lesson and don't call him for a week. If your friends try to say something smart to you, don't do what's expected of you and flip out on them, surprise them and keep your mouth shut. I know it's hard but sometimes you have to do things differently to get things that you never had. Take it from me; you will be the winner of your destiny if you just focus and do the unexpected to get the things you fee that you want in life.

Now That You're Gone

Mama said don't put your hands in the cookie jar/She said, "Son, have control"/She said everything that's/sweet ain't good for you, no/And everything that glitters ain't gold/And now that you're gone I realize (yes I do)/I've lost my soul/And I don't wanna pass the torch/Baby can you give me one more chance

—"Don't Take Your Love Away"—Avant

As women, we always say that a man don't appreciate us until we are long gone or we always say the grass aint always greener on the other side. Well although it is true, it's not only men that don't appreciate a good thing until it's gone; it's us women too.

Growing up my first love did everything I have ever wanted him to do. He went to the stores and bought me pads, he walked 20 blocks to White Castles to get me something to eat, hell, he even saved up money from his $300 and some change check every week just so he could give me all those fancy things that women kill for like Louis Vuitton Purses and Tiffany Jewelry.

Everything was gravy until we started to grow up and things started to switch. Everything that was cute before wasn't that cute anymore and after a while we both just wanted different things. I wanted someone that was a little bit manlier and real good with his hands so that he could fix things for me. I wanted a man that talked back a little more and held his own ground. Hell, I wanted a ride or die dude who would tell his family to fuck off, this is my lady, and don't tell her shit. I wanted someone who made me feel like cooking for him, someone that came over and demanded for me to bend it over, overall be the aggressor in the relationship and I will be the one listening for once in my life. My first love was a really nice guy, real laid back. He was what I called a "Yes Nigga," he said yes to whatever I said. I don't know if it was his demeanor or the fact that he was just young and in love but whatever the case was, it was really getting annoying.

My ex wanted a prissier woman. He wanted someone that didn't curse his ass out for the slightest things like falling asleep during a movie or not coming directly home from getting his haircut. He wanted someone that it wasn't a big deal for her to wear heels while she cooked and just listened to him and play the role of the woman and I just wasn't that type of person.

As you can see we had the same issues most couples have when they are with each other from 15 to 21-years-old. I mean the smallest things were becoming a problem for the both of us. Funny thing is now that I look back and think about his faults; I came up with the conclusion of so what he didn't know how to fix anything, at least he was willing to give me the money to hire someone to do it for me. So what he wasn't very handy, he had other qualities that most men didn't acquire like he was giving, caring, and very responsible.

The truth is I wanted someone to be up my ass all day, everyday, and tell me how great I was, he never really did that, but his actions showed me how great I was. He used to just bring me home flowers just for the hell of it (damn, I really miss those days). I could go on and on about this man because believe me he was something really amazing. Sadly, me being the spoiled brat that I was didn't see how great he was until now. My ex and I was about to break up all the way back in 2003 (two years before the actual break up) and he wrote this email titled *You're Stupid, I'm the Greatest!!!* to me that I have saved in my inbox to this day. Something that he said really struck a spot in my heart. He wrote:

I'm a fuckin catch and I'm mature enough to know that now so have fun with the "niggas that sweat you" cuz in the end that pillow of yours will be drenched in tears thinkin about the kind of man you lost. You may laugh at that now, but give it some time you'll see exactly what I mean. Why couldn't you have just understood my situation??? Why did you always have to bitch??? I loved you from the bottom of my heart and I still do. But, I can't let you do this anymore. Your selfishness will be your downfall in life, REMEMBER THAT!!!!

And just like he said, I read it and laughed but you know what he was right. Many nights after we broke up, I cried plenty of nights all alone with my pillow. I don't know why but after him, I started dating the guys that I just assumed was going to sweat me and think I was so great. I started dealing with guys that I knew wasn't on my level. I guess I wanted to help others become great and as I told you before you can't help these guys because once they're good, they look at you like you never did anything for them in the first place. Remember; don't take people for granted no matter how much you think you may find someone else that's going to do the same thing for you because in the end, you will live to regret it.

Face it, he's broke!

When I was younger I never knew the importance of dating a winner, someone who could help you out during the bad times; I gave all kinds of men a chance to date me. I guess because I thought if you had your own dough, you would never need someone else's. I was young then but now I am grown with grown ass bills and believe in the ideology that if it doesn't make dollars, it doesn't make sense.

Most losers are considered losers because they are broke and being in a relationship with someone who is flat out broke becomes very frustrating after a while. You cant go away to any trips with him because he don't even have his own half of the plane ticket; you wont receive any nice gifts because he cant afford it and he wont be paying as he lay because he's broke. Now what is a broke Dude? No, it's not a guy that only makes $8.00 per hour. It's a guy who has not a dime saved and/or can't tell you the next time his name will be on a paycheck. I once messed with a guy who was so broke that he didn't even have enough money to get on the train to come see me. I cut him off because a man that broke doesn't need pussy; he needs some integrity and a job application.

Men who are broke will always be jealous of the next man who comes around show stopping. They will not feel comfortable around a Diva like you especially when you're dressed all fly with your v-neck chocolate brown dress and matching high heeled sandals and he's simply just rocking a white t-shirt. A broke man will always rather stay inside or make you pay when you want to go on a date. Broke men like being with real motivated women so that they could live off of your ass while they sit and believe that they're the king of your castle. Broke men don't have the value of a dollar. So when he gets a little cash, even though you held him down for six summers, he won't spend a dime on you.

Broke men never remember the people that had them when they were real messed up and ashy. So what happens if you try to get him to step his game up? Good question, right? I did the same thing, I was always *super-save-a-ho* type of chick, and guess what when you do this, when you do this you get screwed in your ass with no Vaseline in the end. There you go filling out job application for your man and running in the rain by yourself to get his bum ass an interview shirt and when he gets that job, what happens? All of a sudden he didn't want to mess with you because he can't take your attitude and think its time for you guys to have some space.

Honey please, its not because he needs space, it's because he has a job now and doesn't need you anymore. That's why it's very important for an independent woman to date a man that is already self-assembled. You have better things to do then sit there and try to get a man to do the things he should have been taught to do from his Mama. It's funny how quick men forget how much you upgraded their ass, hell he didn't even have an email address before he met you.

I know we all don't like to admit it when the person we love is not on our level. We kick, we scream, and we run away from the facts that are placed on the table in front of us. As women, we are always trying to get the impossible out of a man. It's great that you have faith in this man and really believe that he is going to be someone great in the future but face it, he's a freaking loser. It's just like what Lil' Kim said many years ago, "9 out of 10 Niggas aint shit, 1 out of 5 Niggas suck a dick." Who would of known that Lil' Kim was a psychic in the making? But anyway, some men don't want shit and they never will have shit. It's not your fault; it's his fault, and his whole demeanor. He has that devil leaking inside of him and he just doesn't want to do right. He tries to get himself together but it just doesn't work, he always backslides. He's just a terrible excuse for a man.

Just you alone can't save him; you need some help from above so instead of stressing over him, please pray for him. You have been with this man for 4 years and you're still having the same problems with him that you had 4 years ago. Look at him; there's no evolution, no growth, and there's still no money coming from his part. Just a low life still dreaming about a career he may never have because he's not serious about anything going on around him. He's still searching for something within himself that will make him feel whole and complete but he won't even find that because he is already cursed with the mistakes of his absentee father and trifling mother.

Instead of witnessing his problems and making more of himself, he sits there and dwell on the past that still seems hinders him. Girl, you don't need him. He has problems, he has issues, and most of all, and he has no plans to make them better. He just uses his troubles as an excuse. His excuse to be a misogynist, his excuse to be unemployed, his excuse to not like the skin he's in but most of all his excuse to treat you like dirt. Face it or it will face you, he's a loser, get rid of the lame! One thing you must remember about dating a broke man is broke men brings broke problems. That Sexually Transmitted Disease called BMD (Baby's Mama Drama) is a broke problem; not receiving a gift on *Valentine's Day* or *Christmas* is a broke problem; you not being able to talk to your man because he doesn't have any minutes on his pre-paid phone is a broke problem. See being broke equals problems. Not having money can lead to depression, death, insanity, and heart disease; think about it!

When you're broke, you are upset at not only yourself but also the rest of the world. When you're broke, you can't afford to eat so you can die from starvation or kill some innocent soul as you try to rob their ass. When you're broke, you become insane from thinking about how you're going to pay the bills and take care of yourself. All of this broke thinking leads to pressure on your heart, which could lead to a heart attack. So my broke theory is really is true.

We also have to remember that broke men are big users. They expect for you to trick because, hey, you're working. It's very hard to spot one of these users but I am here to help you out. Broke men don't start out by asking you for big stuff, they start out by asking you for small favors like lending them $40 or using your computer to check their email. I broke down users into two different categories, *Sample A and Sample B* so listen up to see if your man fit any of these descriptions. The *Sample A* is the worse kind of user, he's the type of person that you don't really see coming. This man is a beggar and what helps him is his undeniable charm (he will talk you out of your panties).

He's the type of user that calls you plenty of times before he tells you some sob story that is supposed to make you offer up your cash because he doesn't want you to think that he called only because he was in a messed up situation and needed some help. What's aggravating about him is that you will never know when the using will begin; it just comes out of nowhere and hits you. They may spend like $15 on a meal for you but I guarantee you that they will get their money back from you slowly but surely. This type of user has the most game because they spend a little to get a lot. This sort of user loves gullible looking girls so that they can take advantage and milk those pockets. The *Sample A* user will take you out but when the bill comes along he uses excuses like "I got robbed", "I lost my money", or my favorite, "I left my wallet at home." See he has pride so he won't come out blatantly to ask you for money, he will bullshit his way around the fact. The best cure for this man is to let him know that you will not be able to help him the second time around. You have to let him know that this can't go on and that right there will stop him in his trap.

Sample B is a poor excuse of a man because unlike *Sample A* he doesn't have a problem begging. *Sample B* is a different type of user. He's the one who doesn't care who knows he's broke. The inability to hide their begging ways is the downfall of this broke man. Every time you are in need of something his excuse is always he doesn't have it but will be the first person to have his hand out for something. This type of user won't spend any money on you until you're ready to cut him off. This is the kind of guy who expects for you to cook dinner and run bubble baths for him but doesn't come over with the groceries for the food or the soap for the bubbles.

Remember the ones that don't come over with nothing in his hand is more demanding then the ones that do come over with a little something-something. This kind of user has the attitude like *I am broke but you knew this when you met me so don't expect for me to be able to do anything for you.* Don't get fooled by this attitude ladies and feel sympathetic for this user because the day you decide that you cant help him, he will show you how broke he really is not by getting whatever it is that he has asked you for from another person. Getting it anyway is supposed to show you that there are plenty other women out there that are willing to give up that cash. This user is very ruthless. He's the type of person that takes it upon himself and spends your change when you send him to the store. He is a person that will see you with $20 and will ask you for $10. He is a person that doesn't care what 50 Cents says, he still likes to go window shopping. He is just the type of person that looks broke. The best cure for *Sample B* is to let them know from the beginning that you are not having it and they are straight bumming it and they need to get their stuff together. If you met or have a man that may fit in one of these categories, run for your life!

As I preached many of times to my home girls, we deserve more. I don't deserve to be paying for a man's way. I am not short changing myself, I mean some times it's cool to help your man out but it's crazy to let him sit there and never have any dough. I didn't grow up seeing men taking money from females; I grew up seeing a man bring that money home every week. My first boyfriend held it down financially in our relationship as well and never asked me for anything in the whole 6 years. He wasn't a Jay-Z or Lebron James sort of dude but he did believe his girl should have anything that she needed. I respect a regular dude, who don't have big dollars, when he make sure his lady is taken cared than a rich man that does it because the regular dude don't really have it to be shelling out so that's definitely what's up.

My famous line when it comes down to broke men is that you don't need a liability in your life, you need assets. A broke man is a definite liability. If you have a man that's a liability, get rid of his ass (quick). You can definitely do bad all by your goddamn self. Think about it like this, you have two jobs and your man doesn't have one, what you need him for? See everyone thinks like this but they're too afraid to say it aloud. I believe in supporting your man's goals and all but there's a difference between a goal and a goddamn dream. I'm not saying shit on a dude when he's down but I'm saying if he never had nothing to bring to the table in the first place and still doesn't have nothing to bring to the table-he has to go. I know chicks that allow these B.A.D. (Broke Ass Dudes) live with them and they always live to regret it. 6 months down the line this man still don't have his half of the rent. Stay home all day and expect you to come home and cater to their ass. Is he freaking kidding me? If a man doesn't have a job, he should be the one cooking, cleaning, and catering to his woman but I don't recommend you letting your man stay home with no job. You can't possibly respect a man who doesn't bring home some kind of cheddar, I know I can't.

Hell, you can't get your mind right while you're holding down the fort all by yourself; that's too stressful I remember when I had my first real apartment by myself, this guy used to come over and eat cereal. He would eat cereal out of this big ass bowl. I mean this bowl was big enough to feed twelve starving kids in Somalia. I used to look in disgust like how this dude going to come over here and eat this big ass bowl of cereal when he didn't buy the bowl or the box of cereal. In the real world, you have to pay what you weigh. Ladies don't play that big bowl of cereal stuff! That's why ever since then I had this rule: *No man could come over my crib without something in his hand.* That Dude better come over with a bag of groceries, some sodas, some lunch money, something because I'm not that desperate that I'm going to take care of a man just for some dick. Sometimes it's good to be a little selfish. Selfishness helps you get your mind right. It's always displayed as a negative thing but it's actually a good trait to have. I know you don't like to think about yourself and you want to save these broke dudes but like Jada Pickett said in the movie *Jason's Lyric,* "You can't save a person that don't want to be saved."

Ladies, it's time to get back to the old school where we just worried about our families, our health, and ourselves. I know woman who say that don't feel comfortable having their handout but what I have to remind them is that man never has a problem asking you for some coochie. Please, don't worry about how a man would view you if you ask him to help you out a time or two. I don't care about a broke man because a man who doesn't keep money in his pocket doesn't care about himself. I done did the lending money thing before (nothing over $200) and guess what I never saw a dime of my money back. I mean I'm a rider to the end but believe me if you don't take care of them they will find some other dumb ass to do it.

These men always want something for nothing. You go hard, being there for them, sucking them off, buying birthday cakes, and when your birthday comes around, your ass don't even receive a phone call wishing you a happy birthday. He really appreciated you (right!). What these broke asses don't understand is that sometimes it's the little things in life that count. Ok, he's broke but he still could do things that will brighten up your day like he knows your phone bill is $100 and he can't help you pay the whole thing but he should be like, "Hey honey, I know your phone bill is high, so here is $50 towards it." He could even leave a card in your pocket book telling you how much he appreciates how you stick by him through his trials and tribulations, but no he doesn't do any of these things because being broke is his answer to everything and he seems to not think of anything else; yeah right, he's just broke and looking for a hand out and does not care anything about you or your happiness.

So ladies remember that a relationship is a partnership. It is not one sided and you don't owe him anything; you are not his mother. When a guy wants you to take care of him, always think about Halloween; you should never trick or treat. He doesn't care if he's broke so why should you? Remember that everything in this world cost and like my Daddy T always said to my sisters and I whenever we went out on a date, "Don't come home with a wet ass and some Chinese food."

Girl, Get Your Mind Right!

I decided to write this book because I know a lot of pretty, educated, weak women who allow a "mind wrecker" to take over their world. I didn't write this book with the intention to lecture; I wrote it to expose all of the crazy things that these deadbeat men try to do to break a woman down. I didn't want you to read this book thinking that I am getting down on you because you may have not let a man back in your life who you know wasn't shit and that didn't do right by to you because everybody makes mistakes and backslides on their word sometimes.

While writing this book, I backslid and broke some of the rules that I have established. I didn't do it intentionally, it was just I allowed my loneliness to get the best of me and before I knew it, I was back all loved up with the man who I knew was beneath me. I am telling you this not only because my father threatened to write a blog blowing up my mistake but also because I want you to know that a few pitfalls may come along while you are trying to get yourself together.

Believe me, everything is not going to be perfect when you are trying to get yourself together. I went back and slept with a man who tried to hurt my feelings in the past and make me feel low and I did it only out of the past emotions that I had for him. I had many of new men in my life (who I wasn't sleeping with at the time) yet I went back and made love to a man who I knew could never treat me the way that I wanted to be treated. It was wrong for me to take a step backwards but this is something that you can't hear from someone else, this is something that you have to discover for yourself and I had to get my mind right and discover it for myself.

When I went back and slept with him after I erased him out of my mind, my thoughts, and my desires—I felt dirty like a two-dollar hooker looking for her next trick. I felt like everything I have built for myself emotionally came crashing on down. I guess you have to experience that feeling in order to finally get it all together. Your mother could tell you this guy is not good for you, I could tell you, hell, he could tell you but you have to see it for yourself and once you make that decision, you have to stick with your guns and never ever look back. Like many ladies who I have spoken to about ex-lovers, we go back for the feeling of comfort; we go back in hopes that we can rekindle something only to be duped later on down the line.

If any of us want to become self-sufficient, we must leave the past alone and seriously move on (no ifs, ands, or buts about it). It's like what my father told me one night, "You take loose change and put in a jar" and that's some of the best advice he has given to me to this day. Sad but true, we all love abuse. I'm not saying we all like to get our asses whipped or cursed out but I'm saying we love to feel wanted by a person who seems not to want us and I guess that's why after months of building myself up, I went backwards just for 30 minutes of pleasure but don't worry, I'm good now. I loved the way he seemed to hold me and grind inside of me all the while saying he missed me not realizing that if he missed me, he would do anything to make sure he had me and kept me happy. I realized that my pride was taking over because no matter what the next chick said or done, he was back in my bed and what I didn't realize was that he was back not only because he knew where the good stuff was but because it was convenient.

In the end it wasn't about loving Tionna Smalls or about loving his child's mother, it was about him getting in where he fits in. Its like what I always say, a man always seems to come back inside of your life after it seems like you got over him or moved up in the world. He left me as Tionna Smalls, the Administrative Assistant/ Salesperson at a storage facility who dreamed of making more of herself and came back to Tionna Smalls, the young, motivated, entrepreneur headed for greatness with a book on the way. When he left, I was just getting into myself and getting into my own, and when he came back I was confident enough to know that everything I have once dreamed about was finally going to come through. Then it all comes back to when a man is under you on the totem pole and knows that you look good and is doing well for yourself, they try to fuck you just to get a notch on their belt. Its like so what you bad mouthed him to people and called him a bum and said you will never mess with him again, he still came back to you after all those months of being missing in action and fucked and I don't want any of you ladies going through that bullshit.

When it comes down to it, women emotions are all messed up. We love to love and sometimes we just can't let go no matter how hard we try. I don't consider myself an emotional person but at times I think of the past as the present and I just can't get certain people out of my mind. So what stops all of the bullshit from lurking back up? That's the real question in the end. Well what stops all of that is finally being real with yourself and your situation and saying "I'm not taking it anymore". After the last time I backslid, I promised myself I would never again go back on my word. All of the anxiety of catching something from his ass or his chick calling me just started to get me really disgusted. The real name of the game is finally realizing that there is no win when you're dealing with a selfish bastard. I started to look at my success while dealing with men and I started to look at my failures and I realized that I was more successful in almost everything I did in life when I finally realized that I no longer gave a fuck. Not caring about other people is the name of the game. I know it sounds harsh but think about it.

Men are better in this game called love because they may love you but that don't affect their actions (most of the times). It's like so what I have a woman who I love, I like this one and want to see where this could go. They act and don't think about the consequences until later on. It's like why should they think about it when they are the ones benefiting from the situation. So what you're at home crying your eyes out, they're out there doing what they want to do and they don't give a fuck. I also look at the way I treated men after my first love and I broke up. I never called the guy I liked; I waited for him to call. I never offered to see him, I waited for him to initiate seeing me. I never bought them gifts, they spoiled me and I never said I loved them no matter how much I might have had loved them. Its like the less you care, the less you do; the less you do, the more you win and that's in any kind of relationship even a work relationship.

I look at my previous jobs, the person who did the least work, got the most credit. The person who cared the least had the most respect from the boss. It's like if you didn't need the job but worked anyway, you had respect but the person that needed the job always seem to get their ass fired first. I want you to remember one thing from this book and this is some of the best advice you will get from anyone; *so what! shit happens, life is not that serious.*

My life changed for the better once I started to realize this. All these years since I was a little girl in elementary school, I dwelled on stuff that was irrelevant to my life and to my happiness. I dwelled on stupid shit like not fitting into a bra only to have some of the biggest breast you may have ever seen. It's like all those nights of crying because I felt like I didn't fit in were wasted; I could have been doing something else better with my time. I no longer dwell on stuff that I cannot change and that's what you have to do with those *Mind Wreckers* who you've read about in the introduction. If that man did you dirty in the past; so what, shit happens. You may have a broken heart but at least you have your health and that's what is keeping me sane and from killing a few people. Remember in life, no one is perfect and whether we admit it or not, we have all done our dirt in the past. Just like we have been hurt, we have brought hurt to other people. Life is too short for us to think about the coul-das, wouldas, shouldas; We have to focus on what we have now and what we have now is ourselves. I once believed that my first boy-friend and I were going to be together forever. I mean, years have past since we have broken up and people still come up to me assum-ing we got married. I would love to go back to the comfort, the sta-bility, and the time where I felt loved the most but life moved on whether I was ready or not. I can't look at men who are just a little older than I am and expect them to be happy with just me and they too cannot expect the same from me.

All we can do is enjoy people while they're in our lives and hope that every person we come across brings us joy because if they don't we really don't need them in our lives. I know now that as a woman coming up in the 21st century, I must focus on the things that makes me happy that don't have anything else to do with another person; because in reality other people disappoint you but its like what Beyonce' has said in her song, *Me, Myself, and I*, "I know that I could never disappoint myself" and that's the truth. The point of this book is to let you know you would never be happy in your career, your love life, or yourself until you look at you and realize its you that matters the most; not a man, not a new Louis Vuitton purse, and damn sure not money. When I say girl, get your mind right! I'm talking to myself more than I am talking to you. I have come a long way but I have even more ways to go but I want you to look at my path and learn from it and see that this is me, live and in the flesh. I am just like you; I cry when things don't go my way, I feel pain when things don't work out, and most of all, sometimes I feel like a loser but you know what now I am real enough to see when my ass is slipping and when that happens I know how to pull myself back up and take a breath and say, "Ooh, that was a close one."

My name is Tionna Smalls and I thank you for reading this book and prays that this will motivate you for the future but if you read this and slip back into your old ways, I will be back for you. May God bless you and remember it's not what happens to us in our lives that make us who we are; it's what we do after. So remember, when bad things come your way—make sure you fight it and move on. I want you to stay strong, keep yourself as high as a kite, and always if you plan on being successful, to keep your mind right.

10 Tips to Getting Your Mind Right!

1. **Never "Dupe" Yourself**—When you sit there and let a guy do you dirty, you're basically signing your strength away, therefore, your duping yourself. Remember that a man only does what you allow him to do to you.

2. **Stay Strong Even If It Means Being Alone**—yes, it's true, no one wants to be alone but like I said earlier in the book, if a man is doing you wrong, you're alone anyway. Being strong is the beginning of a healthy life and relationship. Remember that a man doesn't define who you are.

3. **Don't Fall Vim to the P.E.N.I.S.**—Yeah we all want it but how much are you willing to risk just to have it? I know it feels good but don't risk your life for 15 minutes of pleasure (if you're lucky). I know he has some good stuff but don't let him do you wrong just because you're horny. Read a book, take a shower, and get over it!

4. **Remember to Forgive but You Never Forget**—In order to move on and have a great life, you must let go of all the hurt and the pain from the past. Moving on will free you from lots of stress and make you more of a fierce chick. There is no such thing as regrets, its just learning experiences. Remember that and you will go far.

5. **Always Keep Yourself Together**—I don't care if you only got $2.00 in your purse, you keep yourself together and always show your best foot forward. Looking good is one step to living a happy and healthy life. It's true that when you look good, you feel good and that's what its all about.

6. **Always Stay Positive**—I don't care about how it's looking now but believe me, it's going to get better. Positive people are successful people and successful people are positive people. Remember that if you think good thoughts, good things will happen to you and that's something we all strive for. Surround yourself with nothing but positive things and I guarantee that you will feel like a better person.

7. **Remember That In the end, All You Have is Yourself**—Don't ever depend on someone else to make you happy mentally, physically, emotionally, and financially; always depend on yourself. I don't care how many people you think you have, remember that when the smoke clears, all you have is you. There is not one person in the world that is going to jump in the casket with you when you die. Try to live your life for yourself. It's a great feeling when you could just sit there and have someone to lean on but you must understand that that same trust you have in them as a support system is the same trust you must have for yourself. No matter what.

8. **Broaden Your Horizons**—You must go out and experience new things if you plan on getting your mind right. Maybe you're meeting all the wrong men because you're closing yourself in one box and not welcoming other great prospects to come into your life. Go and do something you have never done before and watch how quickly life will change.

9. **Don't Worry About What Others Think About You**—Don't worry about it because they don't have a heaven or a hell to put you in. They're going to talk about you regardless whether you're doing good or bad. Remember that they talked about Jesus so you know they're going to talk about you.

10. **Don't Talk About It, Be About It!**—Actions speak louder than words and that saying goes for your life and your career. Many times as women we make the mistake of running our mouths and not doing what we promised ourselves many of times we were going to do. If you say its over-make sure you keep your word to yourself and make sure it's over. Going back on your word only makes you questions yourself. It goes for your career too. If you say you are going to go after your dream and make it happen, godamnit, go after it and make it happen. Women who does what they say they're going to d is more successful in life. Remember that your word is bond.

0-595-45402-X
978-0-595-45402-0

518340LR0